FROM
SALT
TO JAM

For Tom, Lulu, Claude and Eddie.

The beginning and end of everything I do.

Make kitchen magic with sauces, seasonings and more flavour sensations

FROM SALT TO JAM

KATRINA MEYNINK

Hardie Grant

BOOKS

A note about this book

I am not a chef. I never have been. I tried, but the heat, the pace, the stress and the adrenaline were not for me. Food was. Cooking with love was. And sharing was. It all still is, very much so. But that world – the absolute dedication it demands of you to be good at what you do, and the sheer dogged relentlessness of the industry – well, it sucked the joy from everything I loved about food, and so I ran from it and fell into recipe-writing.

Rightly or wrongly, I've been adamant about shooting my own recipes for books. This is my second book where I do so, and I do the same for my column with *Good Food* – all with some understanding editors, it seems. There is no photographer. No stylist. No fancy lights and studios. This is home cooking, cooked in a home.

The plates, the kids, the spoons, the kitchen glimpses – they are all a part of my life. They come from chapters of experience and I feel they give the dishes a sense of place, and a deeply personal one at that.

My grandmother's spoon on one page might be followed by a weathered chopping board made for me by my father-in-law. Or there will be random modern black forks bought in a frenzy before throwing a dinner party for 20 and needing more implements for getting food to mouth. There are ceramics brought back from all corners of the globe by thoughtful friends, and some by local potters and ceramicists committed to their craft.

All of them are important to me. I love them all – the pots, the pans, the plates that have a backstory – but mostly it's the hands that hold them that I treasure most. Because after all, that is the very reason we all cook. To feed those we love.

Dinner is hard ...

It's daily.

No one ever offers to stir away that responsibility; pop it in the oven, call it done and pass you a wine.

I spend my life thinking, cooking and writing about food, but I know the depths of an empty cupboard, the angst that comes with a hungry child screaming for dinner, and I've called cereal a meal on numerous occasions. I've often wondered if I should write a book with chapters titled 'It's okay, no one actually preheats the oven', 'Many mistakes were made', 'Just add loads of cheese', and 'Milo on ice cream makes a wonderful dessert'. But through it all I have always, always believed that food, however it comes, is what binds us. That we need to do what we can to sit together, no matter how briefly, to share a meal.

And the key, my dear friends, is in your condiments. Those bits normally housed unlovingly in the back of your cookbooks collecting dust are where flavour and convenience collide.

If there is one thing I have learnt it is that the finishing touch – the sauce, the relish or the sprinkling of spice – will bring a dish home. It is the glue that binds; the workhorse your dinner grind needs.

This book is a celebration of condiments and seasonings. I want you to flip your thinking and, when prepping or thinking of meals, go to your condiment first. It may seem counterintuitive, but I'll take the opportunity to remind you that a lot of bloody average food has been vastly improved by a decent sauce or a compound butter melting with largesse. Focus on the sauces, the spices and the dressings and the meals will flow from there. Complete, exciting and enticing meals. The kind of meals that encourage chutzpah, sauce-spilling, sharing, surprise and delight.

We are too busy to labour too much over each plate of food we send from our kitchens to the table. Having an arsenal of herb-laced, vinegar-spiced, spicy, sour or sweet salsas, dressings, pastes, jams and more on hand makes it easy to add flavour to a dish quickly, and without much fuss. It keeps the spirit of the food relaxed and not showy while giving your weeknight dinner rotation enough contrast to sustain interest. It will give your cooking a sense of the 'curated amongst the chaos'.

These condiments and spices are a microphone to flavour. They amplify and embrace what is on the plate. You can have the simplest of ingredients and I swear by a decent relish, a sauce that has looked after itself simmering on your stove, or a

beautiful mix of salt and herbs that takes a meal from average to spectacular. Little things can make a big difference in the kitchen.

The following recipes supply you with the condiment or spice first – and then dishes to celebrate them. They will add convenience and return you to the table; while emancipating you from the panic of 'What can I cook for dinner?'. They are a hedonistic mix of salads, comfort foods and dishes to feed your family and friends. They are dishes for celebration, reflection, satisfaction and hibernation. They are the kind of food both to feed and to be fed.

I hope you love them as much as I do.

(above)
Loaded falafel fries (page 183)

One last thing before you get started

In addition to all the condiment glory on the following pages, you'll find that I often incorporate a number of other ingredients. They are bolsters. They add depth, a roundness of flavour or a point of interest to enliven literally any dish. If I don't have them in my cupboard or fridge, I feel naked, exposed. I can't, wont, don't know how to cook without them and I hope you decide you feel the same way. Run forth and stock that pantry immediately.

When in doubt, reach for these:

- Salt. Salt is king

- Garlic. There is never, ever enough

- Butter. Really really good-quality butter

- Lemons (juiced, sliced, grated). A minimum of 3–4 (preferably unwaxed) in your fridge or on your bench at all times

- Parmesan

- Feta, buttermilk, yoghurt (instant richness and acidity)

- Anchovies

- Oyster sauce

- Gochujang and togarashi chilli – so buttery, so rounded in heat

- Aleppo pepper and urfa biber chilli

- Veal jus

- Semi-dried smoked tomatoes

- Yuzu kosho

- Yuzu juice

- Dulche de leche

- Couveture chocolate- all the shades

A note on measurements

All tablespoons used in this book are 15 ml tablespoons. If using a 20 ml tablespoon, use a scant tablespoon and common sense when measuring.

This book isn't a cooking lesson; it's a rough roadmap for flavour-addled dinners. But if I could impress a few simple things that will make you a better cook, they would be:

- *Use scales.* Measure things – definitely always for baking. When you develop and have confidence in your palate, you will find yourself using scales less and less.

- *Taste, taste, taste.* You have to know how a dish is progressing as you cook. It's simply odd not to know if it needs a dash of sugar to temper acidity, a knob of butter to add richness and round out flavour, or the glory of accurate seasoning.

- *Visuals and aroma are two of the most important cues.* I object with every fibre of my being to the inclusion of time in a recipe as a measure of doneness. It's like leaving all your hard work to fate. Who does that in any other setting? Does it smell like it is changing? Does it look like it is changing? Learn the visual and aromatic cues of the foods you cook. Trust. Your. Instincts.

- *All meat should be at room temperature before cooking.* Cold to extreme heat does not result in a well-cooked tender piece of protein.

- *If you think you've stuffed it up, reach for salt or acids and season first.* Next reach for roundness (fats), and sweet last. Unless you've burnt the hell out of it, a lot of mistakes are fixable.

Okay I lied ... just one more thing

Make notes. All over these damn pages. Be completely disrespectful. Change things, adapt things, do things to these recipes that are to your taste. Edit for what you love, sub for what you have on hand, replace for what you hate. Just always write it down. Because there is nothing more upsetting than cooking a mind-blowing meal and forgetting what exactly it was you did to get there.

How this book works

The concept of this book is a focus on condiments and seasonings – an arsenal to help your cooking. There are one or two 'fancy' offerings, a few snacks to have with drinks, but mostly it's the straightforward everyday stuff, the kind of food you might like to come home to or happily make after a busy day. When you have a collection of condiments at hand, something in your pantry or fridge ready to reach for at a moment's notice, it will make your life that little bit easier. It will help you get off the culinary treadmill of repeating dishes and, with any luck, even fuel your curiosity for the new.

Below I have pulled together a few different menus. I have selected four condiments or seasonings to make, then shown you how they can stretch across 14 days' worth of dinners. But you don't even need to take it that far. A wonderful condiment can be used to liven up a simple piece of grilled protein or some roasted veg – goodness knows that is sometimes all we have time for. The key purpose is to have you making a few ingredients into something really great to eat.

HOW MAKING FOUR CONDIMENTS CAN UNLOCK TWO WEEKS OF MEALS

Chicken salt	Green goddess dressing	PREP	Chermoula	Harissa
Pici, kombu butter, chicken salt and parmesan (page 32)		SUN	Chermoula and haloumi lamb meatballs with lemon (page 76)	
Grilled protein (try lamb) served with chermoula saganaki "n" honey (page 68)		MON	Harissa maple-roasted pumpkin with haloumi and burghul salad (page 80)	
Pasta with kale sauce and harissa (page 82)		TUE	Saucy thighs (page 173)	
Green goddess and broccolini with sunflower seed dukkah served with grilled lamb/fish or any protein (page 169)		WED	Seeded chermoula salmon carpaccio (page 70)	
Tomatoes, tarragon oil, stracciatella, chicken salt (page 40) served with your favourite grilled protein.		THU	Charred cos, buttermilk dressing, chicken salt breadcrumbs (page 36) served with your favourite grilled protein	
Roasted maple-glazed pumpkin with chicken salt, burrata and pepitas (page 35)		FRI	Orange, harissa and olive salad (page 87) served with some grilled fish	
Chermoula tomahawk and tomatoes (page 72)		SAT	Sorta crispy chickpeas, green goddess and feta (page 175)	

WEEK 1

WEEK 2

Bagel seasoning

Tahini yoghurt dressing

PREP

Bloody useful red sauce

Jalapeño jam

WEEK 1

SUN	Pan-fried ricotta and spinach gnudi with parmesan and bagel seasoning (page 28)
MON	Spicy roasted cauliflower with herbs, pomegranate and chickpeas (page 184)
TUE	Tuna, jalapeño and yuzu (page 216)
WED	Roasted pumpkin and pickled onion salad with tahini yoghurt dressing (page 181)
THU	Jammy capsicums with feta, basil and bagel seasoning (page 18) served with grilled protein
FRI	Jalapeño-jam-addled fish burritos (page 226)
SAT	Drunk pasta (page 135)

WEEK 2

SUN	Prawn saganaki with feta, fennel and ouzo (page 129)
MON	Corn and chickpea salad with miso jalapeño tahini dressing (page 224)
TUE	She sure is saucy chicken puttanesca (page 127)
WED	Tuna sashimi bowl with yuzu kosho mayo and bagel seasoning (page 26)
THU	Mescal-marinated steak salad with charred pineapple, jalapeño jam and herbs (page 222)
FRI	Loaded falafel fries for when you need to let them feed themselves (page 183)
SAT	Speedy saucy eggs all'amatriciana (page 21)

Kettle furikake   Ultimate ranch dressing

PREP

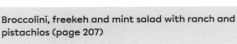 Caramel   Thai-style dressing

WEEK 1

SUN	Life-changing slow-roasted gochujang chicken with furikake butter (page 49)
MON	Soba, seeds and sauce (page 191)
TUE	Cavolo nero, chorizo, preserved lemon with smoked almonds and ranch (page 202)
WED	Furikake Paris mash soup (page 46)
THU	Crunchy cukes with spicy peanut kinda nahm jim (page 196) served with grilled protein
FRI	Tooona noods (page 52)
SAT	Togarashi caramel beef skewers (page 146)

WEEK 2

SUN	Sunday slow-roasted pastrami brisket with ranch, pickles and kettles (page 208)
MON	Roasted carrot and parsnip salad with feta, caramel and crunchy bits (page 141) served with grilled protein
TUE	Crisp chicken, radish pea salad and ranch (page 210)
WED	Thai-inspired beef sub (page 190)
THU	Broccolini, freekeh and mint salad with ranch and pistachios (page 207)
FRI	Last-minute laarb of sorts (page 192)
SAT	Moghrabieh with yuzu kosho butter and furikake parmesan crisp (page 50)

Bagel seasoning

Jammy capsicums with feta, basil and bagel seasoning 18

Speedy saucy eggs all'amatriciana 21

Sir Yeast a Lot (not your average pull-apart) 22

Peach, tomato, basil and haloumi salad with bagel seasoning dressing 25

Tuna sashimi bowl with yuzu kosho mayo and bagel seasoning 26

Pan-fried ricotta and spinach gnudi with parmesan and bagel seasoning 28

Chicken salt

Pici, kombu butter, chicken salt and parmesan 32

Roasted maple-glazed pumpkin with chicken salt, burrata and pepitas 35

Charred cos, buttermilk dressing, chicken salt breadcrumbs 36

Celeriac chips with chicken salt 37

Chicken salt shallot tarte tatin 38

Tomatoes, tarragon oil, stracciatella, chicken salt 40

Kettle furikake

Slow-roasted onions and furikake 44

Furikake Paris mash soup 46

Life-changing slow-roasted gochujang chicken with furikake butter 49

Moghrabieh with yuzu kosho butter and furikake parmesan crisp 50

Tooona noods 52

Petal spice

Sumac-roasted blood plums, yoghurt and petal spice 56

Living-on-the-edge macaron tea cake with petal spice 58

Roasted rhubarb and pistachio frangipane slab tart 60

Flower farm granola 63

Fairy dusts

I am one of those people who will take a mini pot of salt to a restaurant, because I am completely enamoured with the stuff. Salt is not the devil. Salt does not blunt your palate. Salt does not destroy the nuances and subtlety of flavour. A seasoning, done correctly, is the difference between eating in monochrome or eating in the full spectrum of colour. This is all about the glorious sprinkling finish. A range of simple add-ons that inject flavour, texture, sometimes colour, and always a complexity that will take your cooking from meh to yeah.

Bagel seasoning

This seasoning should not be reserved purely for bagels. Hear me out. The more I cook and the more I eat, the more I inherently understand it's the seasoning that takes food from lacklustre to delicious. Sure, it's the ingredients. Sure, it's how you treat them. But proper seasoning is the glue that brings those elements together for all the eating goodness. Done well, it makes food taste more like itself and this is where bagel seasoning comes in. It heightens and complements flavours without overpowering them.

To make 70 g
(2½ oz/½ cup)

1½ tbsp poppy seeds

1½ tbsp sesame seeds

1 tbsp dried minced garlic or garlic powder

1 tbsp dried minced onion

2 tsp sea salt flakes (smoked if you happen to have it)

1 tbsp nutritional yeast flakes

To make 140 g
(5 oz/1 cup)

3 tbsp poppy seeds

3 tbsp sesame seeds

2 tbsp dried minced garlic or garlic powder

2 tbsp dried minced onion

½ tbsp sea salt

2 tbsp nutritional yeast flakes

To make 280 g
(10 oz/2 cups)

6 tbsp poppy seeds

6 tbsp sesame seeds

4 tbsp dried minced garlic or garlic powder

4 tbsp dried minced onion

1 tbsp sea salt

4 tbsp nutritional yeast flakes

Combine all the ingredients in a bowl, then pour into an airtight screw-top jar. Keeps for a few months.

Jammy capsicums with feta, basil and bagel seasoning

This dish is a riot of colour and promise. Eating it feels like an express route to feeling good about yourself. The capsicum and black garlic is roasted low and slow to the brink of collapse. These are good at a barbecue with all manner of proteins, great on a sandwich the next day, or tossed through a salad or thrown on a pizza. And that is my kind of cooking – I'm not interested unless a recipe can follow through with a solid second act.
Serves 6 as part of a spread

1 kg (2 lb 3 oz) red and yellow capsicums (bell peppers)

6 garlic cloves, smashed

6 black garlic cloves, smashed

2 teaspoons aleppo pepper

60 ml (2 fl oz/¼ cup) olive oil

60 ml (2 fl oz/¼ cup) red wine vinegar

60 g (2 oz/1⅓ cup) brown sugar

125 g (4½ oz) Danish feta, sliced into 6 mm (¼ in) thick planks, brought to room temperature

handful of basil leaves

6 tablespoons Bagel seasoning (page 17)

Preheat the oven to 150°C (300°F).

Cut the capsicums into lobes, leaving behind the core, stem and seeds. Add the lobes to a roasting dish with the smashed garlic, black garlic, aleppo pepper, olive oil, vinegar and brown sugar. Give it all a good toss to coat and pop in the oven.

Cook nice and slow for about 1½ hours. A few times during cooking, get in there with a pair of tongs and flip and move things around to ensure a lovely even caramelisation. If it appears to be burning, add a few tablespoons of water, give it a swoosh and keep cooking.

Remove from the oven and taste – you want a nice sweet tang and caramelised flavour to the capsicums. You can adjust the seasoning with brown sugar and red wine vinegar as needed.

Add the feta to the hot dish and let it sit in the juices, getting acquainted with all the flavours and warming itself through to that ultimate cheese-eating temperature, about 5 minutes. Scatter the basil leaves over, then sprinkle with the bagel seasoning.

This is best served like this straight to the table but, if you want to, you can gently transfer to a serving dish – remember to spoon over any residual juices.

Speedy saucy eggs all'amatriciana

Very few dishes can right the world as quickly as some sunshine-hued eggs swimming in flavour-heavy sauce; it is a perfect call to arms for those days you need to feel allllll the feelings. Other than the bagel seasoning to finish, the key to building flavour at warp speed here is the pancetta and smoked semi-dried tomatoes. **Serves 4**

4 slices of sourdough, roughly torn

3 tablespoons olive oil

1 red onion, peeled and diced

150 g (5½ oz) chopped pancetta

3 garlic cloves, peeled and chopped

80 g (2¾ oz/½ cup) smoked
    semi-dried tomatoes, chopped

2 teaspoons aleppo pepper, or
    to taste

400 g (14 oz) tinned crushed
    tomatoes or Bloody useful
    red sauce (page 124)

25 g (1 oz/¼ cup) grated parmesan

4 organic free-range eggs

4 tablespoons Bagel seasoning
    (page 17)

1 tablespoon oregano leaves
    to scatter

Preheat the oven to 180°C (350°F).

Add the sourdough chunks to a roasting tin, then drizzle with 2 tablespoons of the olive oil. Give it a quick toss to coat the bread in the oil, then bake in the oven until lightly browned and crisp, about 5 minutes.

While the croutons are baking, add the remaining olive oil to a large frying pan over medium heat. Once hot, add the onion and pancetta, stirring occasionally until the onion has softened and the pancetta has started to crisp. Add the garlic, smoked semi-dried tomatoes and aleppo pepper and cook until the tomatoes are breaking down a little and the mixture is fragrant. Add the tinned tomatoes to the pan and cook, stirring often to prevent catching. Cook for about 5 minutes or until the mixture has thickened and reduced slightly. Gently push the bread croutons into the tomato mixture. Sprinkle with the parmesan.

Using a wooden spoon, gently create four divots in the tomato mixture. Crack an egg into each divot and cover the pan with a lid. Cook until the egg whites are just set and no longer translucent, but the yolks are still decadent and runny.

Scatter the bagel seasoning and oregano leaves over the top and serve.

Sir Yeast a Lot
(not your average pull-apart)

This bread follows a technique popular in Asia, where you make a *tangzhong* (like a roux). It makes a HUGE difference to the quality of the bread. When you add the tangzhong, the dough retains a higher moisture content, and the resulting bread is light and fluffy with a beautiful crumb. **Serves 8–12**

Tangzhong

20 g (¾ oz) strong flour

100 ml (3½ fl oz) milk

Dough

185 ml (6 fl oz/¾ cup) milk

1 × 7 g (¼ oz) sachet active dry yeast

55 g (2 oz/¼ cup) caster (superfine) sugar, plus an extra pinch

335 g (12 oz) strong flour, plus extra for dusting

pinch of salt

1 large organic free-range egg

55 g (2 oz) unsalted butter, at room temperature, cut into pieces

1 teaspoon rice bran oil or other flavourless oil, for greasing

Filling

185 ml (6 fl oz/¾ cup) Bloody useful red sauce (page 124) (or use a thick store-bought pizza sauce)

150 g (5½ oz/1 cup) shredded mozzarella

50 g (1¾ oz/½ cup) shredded parmesan

50 g (1¾ oz/½ cup) shredded fontina

2 tablespoons extra-virgin olive oil

To make the tangzhong, add the flour and milk to a small saucepan, place over low heat and cook for 2–3 minutes, whisking constantly. The mixture should turn quite thick and paste-like, almost like mashed potato or a very, very thick béchamel. Immediately remove from the heat and scrape into a small bowl to cool.

To make the dough, add the milk to a medium saucepan over low heat. Bring to a gentle simmer until the milk is bubbling. Remove and allow to cool slightly – it needs to be warm to the touch. Add the yeast and a generous pinch of sugar and set aside until the mixture is foamy, about 5–10 minutes.

In the bowl of an electric mixer fitted with a dough hook, add the sugar, flour, salt and egg. Add the tangzhong and yeasted milk mixture and mix on low until the dough is shaggy. Add the softened butter, one piece at a time, mixing until incorporated before adding the next. Increase speed to medium–high and continue to knead the dough until it is tacky and slightly sticky, 5–10 minutes.

Form the dough into a smooth ball and place in a large bowl greased with rice bran oil. Cover with a tea towel (dish towel) and set in a warm spot to prove until doubled in size, about 2 hours (or place in the fridge to prove for at least 8 hours or overnight).

Generously brush a 25–28 cm (10–11 in) cast-iron pan with olive oil. Combine the shredded cheeses in a bowl, then sprinkle ¾ cup of the cheese mixture around the edge of the pan.

Transfer the dough to a lightly floured work surface and roll out to a rectangle, roughly 30 x 50 cm (12 x 20 in). Spread the bloody useful red sauce over the dough, leaving a 2 cm (¾ in) border all the way around the edges. Sprinkle the remaining cheese over the tomato sauce. Roll up the dough lengthways to form a tight roll, pinching along the seam to seal all the way along. Gently place the dough, seam side down, on your work surface and cut it in

To finish

1 large organic free-range egg

1 tablespoon thick (double/heavy) cream

1½ tablespoons Bagel seasoning (page 17)

half. Arrange the halves adjacent to each other. Pinch the ends together at the top and twist the dough pieces over each other, almost like you are going to make a plait, criss-crossing them a few times, bringing the two ends of the twisted dough to form a round loaf. Place in the cast-iron pan and cover again with a tea towel and rest until doubled in size, about 1½ hours.

Preheat the oven to 190°C (375°F). Whisk the egg and cream in a bowl. Brush the mixture generously all over the loaf, then sprinkle over the bagel seasoning.

Bake until the loaf is golden brown, about 45 minutes. Allow the bread to cool in the pan before gently turning it out. You may need a knife to gently prise the bread free. Otherwise, serve directly from the cast-iron pan to plate. Best on the day it is made but you can briefly reheat any leftovers to bring this bread back to full glory.

Peach, tomato, basil and haloumi salad with bagel seasoning dressing

This is a representation of everything that is good about summer. Sweet lightly acidic tomatoes and juicy, succulent peaches with crisp, teeth-squeaking haloumi. It's hands-down one of my favourite things to eat after hot and salty days at the beach. **Serves 4 as part of a spread**

500 g (1 lb 2 oz) mixed medley cherry tomatoes, halved

4 peaches, stoned and sliced

generous handful of basil leaves

1 tablespoon olive oil

180 g (6½ oz) block haloumi, sliced lengthways

Bagel seasoning dressing

5 tablespoons olive oil

2–3 tablespoons Bagel seasoning (page 17)

Make the bagel seasoning dressing by placing the ingredients in a bowl. Stir to combine, then set aside until ready to serve.

Add the tomatoes, peach slices and basil to a serving bowl. Toss very gently to combine – trying to avoid bruising the peach slices.

Add the olive oil to a frying pan over medium–low heat. Add the haloumi and cook for 1–2 minutes or until golden on one side and beginning to soften. Gently flip the slices and cook the other side until golden.

Top the tomato and peach salad with the haloumi and spoon the dressing over the top. Serve immediately.

Bulk it out for last-minute table gatherers

- Add some sourdough croutons
- Add some prosciutto
- Add some grilled chicken, mackerel or lamb

Tuna sashimi bowl with yuzu kosho mayo and bagel seasoning

Before you shake your head at my influencer-friendly 'bliss bowl' ... pause. I promise this is good. It's like eating a summer holiday with 'my body is a temple' vibes and takes about five minutes to assemble. I love the heft of the yuzu and while I would never have thought it would go with Bagel seasoning, it well and truly does. It's a brilliant match of bright and buttery flavours. **Serves 4**

280 g (10 oz/1½ cups) cooked brown rice

300 g (10½ oz) sashimi-grade tuna

1 avocado, stoned and peeled

4 cups shredded Asian-style salad mix

Bagel seasoning (page 17), to serve

Dressing

60 ml (2 fl oz/¼ cup) kewpie mayonnaise

1 tablespoon yuzu kosho

zest of 1 unwaxed lemon

Optional

pickled ginger

soy sauce

For the dressing, combine the ingredients in a bowl. If it seems a little thick, thin it out with a squeeze of lemon juice or more yuzu. Set aside.

Warm the rice. Place it in serving bowls and top with tuna, some avocado and a small handful of Asian salad per serve. Drizzle over the yuzu kosho mayo, generously season with bagel seasoning and serve with pickled ginger and soy sauce on the side, if desired.

Pan-fried ricotta and spinach gnudi with parmesan and bagel seasoning

Everything seems better in Italian. In English these are just dumplings, but in Italian, *gnudi*. To stretch this recipe a little further, you could add some Bloody useful red sauce (page 124), and crisp pancetta. I've included a weight for the spinach, which seems entirely laborious. Just use a couple of big, scurvy-avoiding handfuls – that should do it. **Serves 4**

150 g (5½ oz) baby spinach

500 g (1 lb 2 oz) firm ricotta

2 organic free-range egg yolks

1 tablespoon finely chopped flat-leaf (Italian) parsley

1 tablespoon finely chopped dill

50 g (1¾ oz) parmesan, finely grated, plus extra to serve

200 g (7 oz) or up to 280 g (10 oz) plain (all-purpose) flour

90–120 g (3–4½ oz) unsalted butter

1½ teaspoons oyster sauce

1 tablespoon Bagel seasoning (page 17) per serve

Very, very briefly run the spinach under some running water, then place in large dry frying pan over high heat and cook for about 30 seconds. Transfer the softened spinach to a sieve and press out any excess moisture. Add to a food processor and pulse until coarsely chopped. Turn out into a mixing bowl.

Place the ricotta, egg yolks, herbs and parmesan in a bowl and stir to combine. Add the flour and use your hands to incorporate it – you want to make a dough that has only just come together.

Tip the dough out onto a lightly floured surface and knead lightly until smooth. Divide into three pieces, then roll each piece into a log shape until about 1.5 cm (½ in) in diameter. It will be about 65 cm (26 in) long. Cut into 2 cm (¾ in) lengths and gently squeeze the pieces in the centres to make a shape like a bow tie.

Cook the gnudi in batches in a large saucepan of salted boiling water. They are ready when they all suddenly bob to the surface like happy little life buoys. Transfer with a slotted spoon to a tray.

Place a frying pan over medium heat. Add the butter and, once foaming, add the oyster sauce and stir quickly to incorporate. Add the gnudi and toss until starting to brown and caramelise on the edges. Season to taste, then transfer to serving plates. Sprinkle with the extra parmesan and the bagel seasoning. Serve with additional parmesan and bagel seasoning on the side. Because more is more.

Bagel seasoning

Chicken salt

We now live in a world where nutritional yeast is a condiment and we are all loving fancy quinoa and activated sprouts; a place where the words monosodium glutamate (don't say MSG) are whispered furtively in dark places. So, this feels like a glorious rebellion. Yes, our lives are better for donning smartwatches in the fresh air. But guess what? I made a chicken salt. And it makes food taste like it's alive. Never ever again should chicken salt be relegated to a stash of piping hot fries the morning after the night before. It should go on almost everything.

To make 210 g
(7½ oz/1½ cups)

4 tbsp chicken stock powder

4 tbsp nutritional yeast flakes

4 tbsp garlic powder

2 tbsp sea salt flakes

1 tbsp dried saltbush (omit if unavailable)

2 tsp lemon myrtle powder (or dried lemon thyme)

2 tsp mustard powder

1 tsp curry powder

3 tsp onion powder

2 tsp caster (superfine) sugar

3 tsp celery seeds

3 tbsp sweet smoked paprika

To make 420 g
(15 oz/3 cups)

8 tbsp chicken stock powder

8 tbsp nutritional yeast flakes

8 tbsp garlic powder

4 tbsp sea salt flakes

2 tbsp dried saltbush (omit if unavailable)

4 tsp lemon myrtle powder (or dried lemon thyme)

4 tsp mustard powder

2 tsp curry powder

2 tbsp onion powder

4 tsp caster (superfine) sugar

2 tbsp celery seeds

60 g (2 oz/½ cup) sweet smoked paprika

To make 840 g
(1 lb 14 oz/6 cups)

120 g (4½ oz/1 cup) chicken stock powder

45 g (1½ oz/1 cup) nutritional yeast flakes

120 g (4½ oz/1 cup) garlic powder

8 tbsp sea salt flakes

4 tbsp dried saltbush (omit if unavailable)

8 tsp lemon myrtle powder (or dried lemon thyme)

8 tsp mustard powder

4 tsp curry powder

4 tbsp onion powder

2 tbsp caster sugar

4 tbsp celery seeds

120 g (4½ oz/1 cup) sweet smoked paprika

Combine all the ingredients in a bowl and stir with a fork to ensure the spices are fully incorporated. Pop into a screw-top jar and prepare yourself for deliciousness. This will last for up to 3 months in a screw-top jar in a cool and dark pantry.

Pici, kombu butter, chicken salt and parmesan

The true magic of this dish lies in the combination of kombu butter and the Chicken salt meeting a rain shower of parmesan. This is the stuff of midnight feasts, desires for comfort, and last-meal requests. After a long, busy week, the therapy of hand-rolling pici is unbeatable. If you need this for a midweek hit, just replace with some great store-bought fresh pasta. **Serves 2–4**

Pici

400 g (14 oz) 00 flour or plain (all-purpose) flour

200 ml (7 fl oz) warm water

1 tablespoon extra-virgin olive oil, plus more for shaping

semolina, for dusting

Kombu butter and parmesan

50–100 g (1¾–3½ oz) unsalted butter (or enough to adequately cover your pasta)

1½ tablespoons liquid kombu

2 tablespoons Chicken salt (page 31), plus extra to season

grated parmesan, to serve (generously)

For the pici, add the flour to a large bowl and make a well in the centre. Add the water and olive oil. With a fork, whisk a small portion of the flour, a little at a time, from the well's inner rim into the liquid centre, until a shaggy dough forms. Knead vigorously until dough is smooth and firm, 10 minutes. Cover tightly in plastic wrap and rest at room temperature for 1 hour.

Cut off a quarter of the dough (cover the rest) and flatten it with the palm of your hand. Using a rolling pin, roll the dough out until about 5 mm (¼ in) thick. If the dough looks to be pulling, brush it with a very light coating of olive oil to prevent it drying and cracking.

Cut the dough into 5 mm (¼ in) wide strips then, using your hands, roll into thin strands. Start in the centre and use your fingers and palms to stretch and roll the dough. Pici is meant to be rustic – you are not aiming for evenly rolled perfection here. Keep in mind that the pasta will absorb some water as it cooks and will swell a little in size. Cover pici and repeat with remaining dough.

Bring a pot of water to the boil. Salt your water so it tastes like the sea. Drop in the pici and cook until it floats to the surface – depending on how thickly it has been rolled, this can take between 2 and 5 minutes. Taste and check for bite but no residual flour-like taste.

While the pasta is cooking, add the butter to a large saucepan over medium heat. Cook, until the butter is beginning to foam. Remove from the heat and stir in the liquid kombu.

Working quickly, strain the pasta, add it to the kombu butter in the pan and add the chicken salt. Using tongs, gently mix to coat the pasta in the butter mixture. Taste and adjust the chicken salt.

Transfer to bowls. Grate over some parmesan (generously) and give each serve another smattering of chicken salt. Serve immediately.

Roasted maple-glazed pumpkin with chicken salt, burrata and pepitas

This is your culinary bulletproof vest for when you need the kind of side that will outshine the main or morph into the main itself. It's the perfect friend to a simple piece of grilled protein during the week, and spectacular lunch arsenal come the weekend. **Serves 4**

1 kg (2 lb 3 oz) butternut pumpkin (squash), sliced into even-sized wedges

2 tablespoons olive oil

1 tablespoon maple syrup

4 tablespoons Chicken salt (page 31)

1 ball burrata (approx. 150 g/ 5½ oz), at room temperature

30 g (1 oz/¼ cup) toasted pepitas (pumpkin seeds)

Preheat the oven to 180°C (360°F). Line a large baking tray with baking paper.

Spread out the pieces of pumpkin in a single layer on the prepared baking tray. Drizzle the olive oil and maple syrup over the pumpkin, then season with salt and freshly ground black pepper and 1 tablespoon of the chicken salt. Toss to coat. Roast in the oven for 40–50 minutes or until the pumpkin has caramelised around the edges and cooked through.

Carefully transfer the pumpkin to a serving platter. Tear the burrata over the hot pumpkin; it will ooze everywhere inappropriately – this is exactly what we want. Scatter with the pepitas and remaining chicken salt and serve immediately.

Charred cos, buttermilk dressing, chicken salt breadcrumbs

This is a salad that is as simple as it is delicious. There is lettuce buried under a cascade of crisped breadcrumbs, and if you've already got a batch of Ultimate ranch dressing (page 201) on the go – this takes mere moments to throw together. The Chicken salt breadcrumbs keep wonderfully in an airtight container for snack attacks, as well as being ready to play 'the finishing touch' to any number of dishes from salad to soup. **Serves 4–6 as part of a spread**

4 baby cos (romaine) lettuces, washed and halved

olive oil, for brushing

4 teaspoons Chicken salt (page 31)

125–250 ml (4–8½ fl oz/½–1 cup) Ultimate ranch dressing

Chicken salt breadcrumbs

60 ml (2 fl oz/¼ cup) olive oil

200 g (7 oz/2½ cups) fresh sourdough crumbs

3 tablespoons Chicken salt, or to taste

2 tablespoons finely chopped flat-leaf (Italian) parsley

Heat a chargrill pan over medium heat. Brush the cos lettuce with olive oil, sprinkle with the chicken salt and cook in the pan, cut side down, until charred, 2–3 minutes. Turn and grill the other side for 2–3 minutes, then transfer to a large serving dish.

While the lettuce is charring, place a frying pan over medium heat to make the chicken salt breadcrumbs. Add the olive oil and, once shimmering, add the sourdough crumbs and cook, stirring constantly until golden. Remove from the heat and add to a bowl with the chicken salt and parsley.

Drizzle over the ultimate ranch dressing – don't drown it, you want just enough for it to nestle delightfully amongst the lettuce crevices. Scatter generously with the chicken salt crumb and serve.

Time hacks

- Use a good-quality store-bought buttermilk dressing instead of the ranch.
- Skip the grilling of the cos lettuce – it's also delightful as nature intended.

Celeriac chips with chicken salt

This is where 'snacks with drinks' begins and ends. I've deep-fried these and burnt them more times than I care to admit, so it's an oven-baked version here and, honestly, these are just as good. Serve with beer and/or a dirty martini. **Serves 1, or 8 as a snack**

½ large celeriac, washed and peeled, ends trimmed

35–70 g (1¼–2½ oz/¼–½ cup) Chicken salt (page 31), or to taste

2 tablespoons olive oil

Preheat the oven to 170°C (340°F). Line two large flat baking trays with baking paper.

Using a vegetable peeler, peel strips of celeriac. Don't be concerned how you do this as the chips shrink and change shape so much in the oven. The key is to keep the strips relatively the same thickness for even cooking. Add the chips to a bowl with the olive oil and toss to coat. Add 1–2 tablespoons of the chicken salt and toss again. (You only want a light smattering of the chicken salt here otherwise it just burns in the oven.) Spread the strips out in a single layer on your baking trays.

Cook, turning at least twice, for 20–25 minutes or until the chips have shrunk, turned golden in colour and are crisp. These chips will continue to firm as they cool. Once thoroughly cooled, toss with the remaining chicken salt. Some will be crispy; some will be mildly chewy. You will become completely addicted.

Chicken salt shallot tarte tatin

Crispy sweet 'n' salty things are an addiction. It's a thing. This tarte tatin should also be a thing. Slow-cooked jammy onions, puff pastry and Chicken salt. This is flavour-chasing at its finest. When is French-inspired food ever a bad thing? **Serves 4**

3 tablespoons chicken stock

3 tablespoons Chicken salt (page 31), plus extra to serve

2 teaspoons olive oil

3 tablespoons brown sugar

350 g (12½ oz) French shallots, peeled and halved lengthways

1 × 375 g (13 oz) sheet puff pastry

Preheat the oven to 150°C (300°F).

Add the stock, chicken salt, olive oil and brown sugar to the base of a 25 cm (10 in) non-stick ovenproof frying pan and give it a quick stir to combine. Add the shallots, cut side up. Cover the pan with foil and roast in the oven for 1 hour. Remove the pan from the oven and increase the heat to 180°C (360°F).

Remove the foil and, using a pair of tongs, turn the shallots over and arrange them in the centre of the frying pan – they will have shrunk during cooking time.

Gently encase the shallots in the sheet of pastry, tucking the edges snugly around the shallots like you would put a small child to bed. Return the pan to the oven and cook until the pastry looks light and golden and has puffed, roughly 20–30 minutes.

Remove the pan from the oven and place a large serving platter upside down on top of the frying pan. Carefully flip the pan and plate over together so the tarte tatin transfers to the plate. There will be hot jammy liquid, so be careful doing this. It is inescapable. Sprinkle with a little more chicken salt and serve piping hot.

Tomatoes, tarragon oil, stracciatella, chicken salt

The glory of this recipe lies in summer tomatoes. It's a total crowd-pleaser for mere moments of labour. The 'effort' is making the tarragon oil but, like the Chicken salt, it's a cracker to have in your summer salad repertoire. The basic rule of thumb is to combine equal parts tarragon, parsley and olive oil. It should be served at room temperature to maximise the flavour of each element. **Serves 4–6 as part of a spread**

250 g (9 oz) stracciatella cheese

3 in-season kumato tomatoes, sliced, plus ½ tomato for juicing

1 × 250 g (9 oz) punnet sweet cherry tomatoes, halved

2–3 tablespoons Chicken salt (page 31), or to taste

Tarragon oil

¾ cup tarragon leaves

¾ cup flat-leaf (Italian) parsley leaves

iced water

185 ml (6 fl oz/¾ cup) extra-virgin olive oil

For the tarragon oil, bring a medium saucepan of water to the boil. Salt well, as you would pasta water, and blanch the tarragon and parsley leaves briefly, until bright green, about 15–30 seconds. Drain, then transfer to a bowl of iced water. Drain once more, then pat with a clean cloth to remove as much water as possible. Add to a food processor with the olive oil and purée until very smooth, this will take about a minute. Strain through a sieve lined with a piece of muslin (cheesecloth) or a clean kitchen cloth will also do a great job. Discard the leaves and transfer the beautiful green oil to a sterilised jar. It keeps, refrigerated for a few weeks – just bring to room temp before using.

Spread the stracciatella across a serving plate. Top with the sliced tomatoes and squeeze over a touch of juice from the extra half tomato as if you are squeezing a lemon over a dish. Drizzle the tomatoes with some tarragon oil and sprinkle with the chicken salt. Serve at room temperature for perfect eating goodness.

Chicken salt

Kettle furikake

I only want to cook dishes that pursue deliciousness above all else. My recipes tend to mish and mash, and go high and low in the blink of an eye. This Kettle furikake is a perfect example of that. Blending buttery, salty potato chips with the traditional furikake blend of flavours is unashamedly delicious. It is a disruptor; a much-needed, take-a-moment interruption for your palate before you resume normal eating. It adds a creamy, crunchy, salty funk and a brilliant injection of flavour to so many recipes. You are going to love it.

To make 270 g
(9½ oz/1½ cups)

50 g (1¾ oz/⅓ cup) combined black and white sesame seeds

1 sheet nori

75–100 g (2¾–3½ oz/3–4 cups) salt and pepper–flavoured potato kettle chips (crisps)

½ tbsp salt flakes

1½ tbsp gochugaru (Korean chilli flakes)

2 tbsp store-bought fried shallots

1 tbsp garlic powder

To make 540 g
(1 lb 3 oz/3 cups)

100 g (3½ oz/⅔ cup) combined black and white sesame seeds

2 sheets nori

200 g (7 oz/8 cups) salt and pepper–flavoured potato kettle chips (crisps)

1 tbsp salt flakes

3 tbsp gochugaru (Korean chilli flakes)

4 tbsp store-bought fried shallots

2 tbsp garlic powder

To make 1.08 kg
(2 lb 5 oz/6 cups)

200 g (7 oz/ 1 cup) combined black and white sesame seeds

4 sheets nori

400 g (14 oz/16 cups) salt and pepper–flavoured potato kettle chips (crisps)

2 tbsp salt flakes

6 tbsp gochugaru (Korean chilli flakes)

8 tbsp store-bought fried shallots

4 tbsp garlic powder

Add all the ingredients, except for the gochugaru, to a food processor or blender and blitz to combine. It's important not to blitz the gochugaru with the other ingredients – it turns the mix a weird red/orange colour so simply stir this through at the end to ensure you get that lovely variation in colour and texture. Lasts for up to 1 month in a tightly sealed screw-top jar.

I've also made this with salt and vinegar kettle chips – also a clear winner. In reality you could try any potato chip, even a packet of corn chips and see where it takes you. I encourage you to try it.

Slow-roasted onions and furikake

I object with the fire of a thousand suns to the concept of a side dish. 'Just sides' make for the best kind of meals – both in restaurants and at home. So here, loud and proud, these onions are in fact a meal. A pretty darn glorious one no less. I'd happily eat them on their own but they're also excellent with warm sticky rice or grilled steak. This is the OG of onions. Take to it with a spoon. **Serves 2–4**

Fairy dusts

10 small onions, halved

2 tablespoons white miso

2 tablespoons brown sugar

60 ml (2 fl oz/¼ cup) olive oil

1 tablespoon Kettle furikake (page 43), plus 3–4 extra tablespoons to scatter

Base

1 tablespoon ponzu

125 g (4½ oz/½ cup) crème fraîche

125 ml (4 fl oz/½ cup) kewpie mayonnaise

For the ponzu creamy concoction base, place the ingredients in a bowl. Whisk with a fork to combine and set aside.

Preheat the oven to 180°C (360°F).

Bring a pot of water to the boil. Add the onions to the boiling water, reduce the heat and simmer for 20 minutes – this speeds up the cooking process and also ensures the onions steam as well as roast when you transfer them to the oven.

Transfer the onions to a roasting tin with tongs – be careful as the onions will be soft and you want to keep the petals in place as much as possible.

Combine the miso, brown sugar, olive oil, kettle furikake and 3 tablespoons of water in a bowl and whisk with a fork to incorporate. Drizzle the mixture over the onions, then roast, uncovered, in the oven for 40–50 minutes. You want the onions to be coloured, completely soft, and the liquid reduced so it's nice and sticky.

Dollop a generous swirl of the crème fraîche mixture onto a serving plate, top with the onions and scatter the kettle furikake over the top. Serve warm.

Furikake Paris mash soup

I planned on making mash and ended up with soup and it tasted so perfectly glorious that there was no going back. Accidents often result in the best of meals. This is basically liquified Paris mash and it's so indulgent and silky and luxurious that I see it being eaten in stretchy pants on the couch, phones off, curtains drawn, the world kept at bay. I equally see it doled out in fancy wee cups as a delicious start to any meal where the need to be *fannnccccaaay* beckons. It's completely and utterly worth it. **Serves 8–12**

1.2 kg (2 lb 10 oz) medium-starch potatoes, peeled and quartered

200 g (7 oz) unsalted butter

2 tablespoons oyster sauce

250 ml (8½ fl oz/1 cup) pouring (single/light) cream

125 ml (4 fl oz/½ cup) chicken stock, warmed

big pinch of salt

1 tablespoon Kettle furikake (page 43) per serve, plus extra to serve on the side

Bring a large pot of water to the boil. Add the quartered potatoes and cook until soft, about 15 minutes. Strain, then return the potatoes to the pot and return to the stove over medium heat. Mash with a fork or potato masher, using the dry heat to remove any residual steam from the potatoes. Remove from the heat.

Add the butter to the pan and roughly incorporate it with your fork or masher, then add the oyster sauce and finally the cream, continuing to mash until you have a chunky-looking soup. Add the stock and a pinch of salt, then pour the lot into a blender and give it a blitz for 15–20 seconds. This will emulsify the soup and make it gloriously glossy and consistent in texture. You don't want to overwork the potato so the residual starch turns this into creamy glue. As as soon as you see it incorporate – turn it off. Taste and check for seasoning. Adjust with salt if needed.

Pour into bowls, then top with 1 tablespoon of kettle furikake per serve.

Enjoy the praise.

And always have extra furikake to serve on the side.

Fairy dusts

Life-changing slow-roasted gochujang chicken with furikake butter

Please welcome to your world the slow-roasted chicken. You are virtually guaranteed a good outcome, no matter what luck-of-the-draw bird you have purchased. It is slow-roasted reliable perfection. The slow-roast answers all our hopes and dreams, with no weird under bits and no tough breasts. Expect perfectly crisp skin, tender fall-off-the-bone meat, and intensely salty, savoury chicken juices to scoop over and give the bird that glorious sheen. **Serves 4–6**

1 organic free-range chicken (about 1.5 kg/3 lb 5 oz)

1 tablespoon gochujang paste

2 tablespoons Kettle furikake (page 43), plus an extra 2 tablespoons to serve

60 g (2 oz) excellent-quality unsalted butter

Gochujang mayo

1½ tablespoons gochujang paste (or to taste)

125 ml (4½ oz/½ cup) kewpie mayonnaise

Preheat the oven to 160°C (320°F).

Place the chicken on a large rimmed baking tray and season with salt. Be generous all over and in the cavity as well.

Combine the gochujang, kettle furikake and butter in a bowl and mix to form a paste.

Using your fingers, gently loosen the skin of the chicken and push the butter mixture gently under the skin and spread it across the meat as evenly as you can. This is a rather messy process but a fundamental flavour step. Be careful not to tear the skin.

Roast the chicken for 2½–3 hours. If you wiggle the legs with a pair of tongs, they should feel like they will almost slip off. It helps to baste the chicken at least a few times with the run-off sauce – collect it in a spoon and pour it back over the chicken as it cooks. It just adds to the flavour and helps to keep the meat as succulent as possible.

While the chicken is cooking, make the gochujang mayo by combining the gochujang and kewpie mayo in a bowl.

Serve the chook with the gochujang mayo and sprinkle with more of the kettle furikake – because more is more in this case.

Kettle furikake

Moghrabieh with yuzu kosho butter and furikake parmesan crisp

This is the kind of dish that fires up all your tastebuds simultaneously. I've made it with moghrabieh (a type of pearl couscous), which maintains its shape and holds the most spectacular chew. The end texture of the dish is quite creamy and loose, but as you add the parmesan it will continue to thicken as it cools. Don't be alarmed if it seems soupy, as this will change in the blink of an eye. You can replace the moghrabieh with Israeli couscous, but be mindful it will need less cooking time. **Serves 4 (just)**

3 tablespoons olive oil

1 large clove of Russian garlic (or 4 regular garlic cloves), thinly sliced

25 g (1 oz) unsalted butter

zest of 1 unwaxed lemon, plus juice of ½–1 lemon, or to taste

250 g (9 oz/1¼ cups) moghrabieh

2 teaspoons yuzu kosho

250 ml (8½ fl oz/1 cup) chicken stock

75 g (2¾ oz/¾ cup) finely grated parmesan

Kettle furikake (page 43), to season

Furikake parmesan crisp

4 tablespoons grated parmesan

2 teaspoons Kettle furikake

Preheat the oven to 180°C (360°F).

Place the oil in a large pot over medium heat. Once hot, add the garlic and butter. Cook until the butter is foaming, and the garlic has softened but not yet browned, about 5 minutes. Add the lemon zest and the moghrabieh and cook for 1–2 minutes. Add the yuzu kosho, stir to coat, then pour over the stock and 400 ml (13½ fl oz) water. Turn the heat to low and simmer for 20–25 minutes, stirring very regularly to prevent catching.

Meanwhile, make the crisp by adding the parmesan in an even layer to a baking tray lined with baking paper. Cover with kettle furikake and cook for 10 minutes in the oven or until the edges are browning and it has taken on a 'crisp' appearance. Remove and allow to cool completely on the tray. Break into shards and set aside.

Add the lemon juice to taste to the moghrabieh mixture, then remove from the heat and stir the parmesan through. Check for seasoning, then scoop into serving bowls. Sprinkle with a hefty pinch of kettle furikake, then top with broken pieces of furikake parmesan crisp. Serve piping hot.

Tooona noods

I have total respect for the multitude of meals and applications a humble tin of tuna (aka the toons) can provide. My only point, and it's a strong one, is that you should cook with tuna in oil only. Anything that says 'spring water' or 'salt-free' or 'tuna in brine' – drop it and *run*. That stuff is rubbish. You deserve better and this recipe deserves better. It's toona. It's a packet of noods. It's the last-minute meal you need in your life. **Serves 2**

1 sheet nori cut into bite-sized pieces

1 × 270 g (9½ oz) packet soba noodles

300 g (10½ oz) tuna in oil (if you can get smoked tuna in oil, which is readily available in supermarkets, I suggest you do), drained

1 avocado, sliced (optional)

3 tablespoons Kettle furikake (page 43), to finish

2 tablespoons thinly sliced spring onion (scallion)

Dressing

2 tablespoons sesame oil

2 tablespoons rice bran oil (or other flavourless oil)

1 tablespoon mirin

1 tablespoon soy sauce

1 tablespoon sake

1 teaspoon white miso

1 tablespoon sweet soy

For the dressing, add all the ingredients to a bowl and whisk to combine. Set aside.

Bring a large pot of water to the boil. Add the nori to a bowl and use a ladle to transfer just enough of the boiling water to cover. Let it soak for 10 minutes, drain, then cool. Set aside.

In the same pot of boiling water cook the noodles according to the packet instructions.

Strain the noodles, then add to a large bowl with the nori and three-quarters of the dressing. Toss gently to coat using tongs. Divide the noodles between bowls. Drain the tuna from the oil, add to the bowls, then drizzle with the remaining dressing. Add the sliced avocado (if using), the sliced spring onion and kettle furikake.

You can serve this hot, cold, warm. However it happens. And people large and small always seem to enjoy it.

Life-is-tough Noodle B

- Hot tip if you just can't do it. Some 2-minute ramen noodles cooked in boiling water, strained and tossed with a touch of butter, then doused in kettle furikake makes for an absolutely spectacular meal. Eaten from your lap is the only way to do it. I aim for about 20 g (¾ oz) butter per individual packet of ramen noodles.

Petal spice

This fragrant, soft and sensual spice mix with floral accents has a grounded, gloriously husky heat. It's a menagerie of flavour that pushes a traditional ras el hanout blend into sweet territory.

To make 20 g
(¾ oz/½ cup)

¼ tsp allspice

2 tbsp ground cinnamon

1 tbsp ground ginger

1 tsp dried fennel seeds

½ tsp pink peppercorns

½ tsp ground turmeric

½ tsp ground nutmeg

pinch of saffron threads

3 tbsp dried edible flower petals

½ tsp ground cumin

½ tsp ground cloves

2 tsp ground cardamom

1 tbsp dried rose petals

To make 40 g
(1½ oz/1 cup)

½ tsp allspice

4 tbsp ground cinnamon

2 tbsp ground ginger

2 tsp dried fennel seeds

1 tsp pink peppercorns

1 tsp ground turmeric

1 tsp ground nutmeg

generous pinch of saffron threads

6 tbsp dried edible flower petals

1 tsp ground cumin

1 tsp ground cloves

4 tsp ground cardamom

2 tbsp dried rose petals

To make 120 g
(4½ oz/3 cups)

1½ tsp allspice

90 g (3 oz) ground cinnamon

6 tbsp ground ginger

2 tbsp dried fennel seeds

1 tbsp pink peppercorns

1 tbsp ground turmeric

1 tbsp ground nutmeg

1 tbsp saffron threads

60 g (2 oz/1½ cups) dried edible flower petals

1 tbsp ground cumin

1 tbsp ground cloves

3 tbsp ground cardamom

6 tbsp dried rose petals

Mix all the ingredients together in a small jar. Seal, then let it sit overnight at least, so the aromatics get well acquainted. Store in a cool dark place out of direct sunlight. Will keep for a few months in a screw-top jar. Give the jar a good shake before using as the finer spices tend to settle at the bottom and you want a lovely, evenly distributed mix.

Sumac roasted blood plums, yoghurt and petal spice

I mean look at this dish. It's so beautiful. It could be breakfast. It could be dessert. In an ideal world, it is both on the same day. You can use sweetened or unsweetened yoghurt here – just run with your preference. If you do use sweet, make sure it isn't sickly. It's lovely to have the variation in sweet and tart flavours. **Serves 2-3**

400 g (14 oz) blood plums, halved (keep stones in)

100 g (3½ oz) caster (superfine) sugar

1 tablespoon vanilla bean paste

2½ teaspoons sumac

375–500 g (13 oz–1 lb 2 oz/ 1½–2 cups) thick vanilla bean yoghurt

4 tablespoons Petal spice (page 55)

Preheat the oven to 160°C (320°F).

Put the plums in a roasting dish (don't take out the stones) with the sugar and vanilla bean paste. Sprinkle the sumac in and mix everything together.

Bake for approximately 20 minutes or until the plums are just soft. Remove the dish from the oven and gently remove the stones from the plums.

Serve three to four plum halves with some yoghurt, drizzling over any residual plum juice from the baking tray. Sprinkle over the petal spice and serve.

Living-on-the-edge macaron tea cake with petal spice

I call this 'living-on-the-edge' as there is no way of ascertaining if the cake underneath is cooked through until you slice it. It forces you to live a little and trust your instincts (along with the baking gods). To that end, it does need to be handled with care, but let your senses guide you. The meringue top should have the lightest, barely sun-kissed tan when ready. And if you shuffle the tin ever so lightly it should have the merest wobble.

Makes 1 x 23 cm (9 in) cake, 10–12 slices

200 g (7 oz) plain (all-purpose) flour

1½ teaspoons baking powder

½ teaspoon salt

150 g (5½ oz) unsalted butter, softened

230 g (8 oz/1 cup) caster (superfine) sugar

3 large organic free-range eggs

1 heaped teaspoon vanilla bean paste

150 g (5½ oz) crème fraîche

10 g (¼ oz/¼ cup) Petal spice (page 55), plus extra for dusting

Meringue

2 large organic free-range egg whites

200 g (7 oz) caster (superfine) sugar

1 tablespoon rosewater

Preheat the oven to 180°C (360°F). Grease and line a 23 cm (9 in) round loose-bottomed cake tin with baking paper.

Sift together the flour, baking powder and salt in a bowl.

In the bowl of a stand mixer fitted with the paddle attachment, cream the butter and caster sugar on medium speed until pale and fluffy. Don't rush, this step is critical to a light, aerated sponge and is where your cake will get all its lightness and lift.

Scrape down the sides of the bowl then add the eggs, one at a time, beating well to incorporate after each addition, then beat in the vanilla. Set the mixer speed to low. Add half the dry ingredients and, when just incorporated, add the crème fraîche and finish with the remaining dry ingredients. Mix until light and aerated. Gently stir through the petal spice before adding to the prepared tin.

For the meringue, add the egg whites to a clean bowl of a stand mixer fitted with the whisk attachment. Whisk on medium speed until foamy, then add the sugar, a tablespoon at a time. Continue to whisk until thick and glossy, then whisk in the rosewater. Dollop the meringue mixture gently onto the surface of the cake batter, then give the top a gentle swirl.

Bake for 45–50 minutes until the top appears a little cracked and is just the palest of caramel colours. Let the cake cool in the tin for at least 20 minutes before transferring to a wire rack to cool. Finish with a generous dusting of petal spice.

Petal spice

Roasted rhubarb and pistachio frangipane slab tart

I love anything in slab form involving pastry. It's the pâtissier's version of a builder's tea. Unpretentious, hardworking, and completely and entirely loveable when shared around a kitchen table. I love the crunch from the crystallised rose petals sitting dramatically aloft the sweet that lies beneath. You can prepare the rhubarb and the petals ahead of time to make this recipe quicker on the day of assembly. **Serves 8–10**

1 × 375 g (13 oz) (approx.) sheet butter puff pastry

500–700 g (1 lb 2 oz–1 lb 9 oz) rhubarb stalks

4 tablespoons Petal spice (page 55)

4 tablespoons caster (superfine) sugar

2½ tablespoons rosewater

Pistachio frangipane

125 g (4½ oz) unsalted butter, softened to room temperature

115 g (4 oz/½ cup) caster (superfine) sugar

165 g (6 oz/1½ cups) ground pistachios

25 g (1 oz) Petal spice

2 large organic free-range eggs

2 teaspoons vanilla bean paste

pinch of salt

35 g (1¼ oz/¼ cup) plain (all-purpose) flour

Crystallised rose petals (optional)

organic, spray-free fresh rose petals

1 organic free-range egg white, lightly beaten

60 g (2 oz) caster (superfine) sugar

To make the crystallised rose petals, brush each petal with the egg white, then sprinkle with caster sugar on both sides. Place on a baking paper-lined tray and set aside for 2-4 hours or until completely dry.

Preheat the oven to 180°C (360°F).

Combine the rhubarb, half the petal spice, sugar, rosewater and 2 tablespoons water in a roasting tin, that fits the rhubarb snugly, then roast until just tender, 10–12 minutes. Allow to cool.

For the pistachio frangipane, in the bowl of a stand mixer fitted with the paddle attachment, beat the butter and caster sugar on medium speed until creamy, about 3 minutes. Add the ground pistachios and petal spice and beat until combined, then beat in the eggs, one at a time, until incorporated. Beat in the vanilla and salt. Lower the speed and add the flour. Once incorporated, turn the speed to medium–high and continue to beat until a light and aerated-style cream has formed.

Line a large baking tray with baking paper. Roll out the sheet of pastry with a rolling pin – you want it stretched slightly so there is a small overhang when you place it on the tray. Gently transfer the pastry to the tray and fold the overhanging pastry back in on itself to create a pastry border about 2–3 cm (¾–1¼ in) wide along all four sides.

Cut a sheet of baking paper to fit inside the border and cover this with pastry weights (or a smaller tray, weighted) and blind bake for 10–15 minutes or until the border has puffed and crisped and the base has started to cook without puffing. Gently remove the weights and return to the oven for another 5 minutes or until the base section is lightly golden. This will prevent your tart from having a soggy bottom. It should be crisp to the touch. Let cool.

Spread the internal section of the pastry with the pistachio frangipane. Strain the rhubarb from any liquid. Line the roasted rhubarb over the frangipane, fitting the pieces as snugly as possible. Scatter the remaining petal spice over the top and bake in the oven for 20–30 minutes. You want the edges to have puffed and be completely golden. The rhubarb will have shrunk slightly, and you should see little slivers of pistachio frangipane peeking through.

Remove from the oven and scatter with a smattering of petal spice and the crystallised rose petals, if desired. Serve warm or at room temperature. Best eaten on the day of making.

Flower farm granola

Some call this a cereal. I call it lovely. Whatever you want to call it, this granola has the audacity to improve your breakfast and/or snacking game. It has the golden hue of sunsets and just the right amount of crunch without breaking your teeth. Because it's made without any nasties, it can soften over time. Simply rebake in the oven for 10 minutes to bring it back to optimal condition. **Makes 8–10 cups**

300 g (10½ oz/3 cups) rolled (porridge) oats

115 g (4 oz/¾ cup) almonds

50 g (1¾ oz/¼ cup) pepitas (pumpkin seeds)

115 g (4 oz/¾ cup) cashew nuts

55 g (2 oz/1 cup) flaked coconut

5 g (⅛ oz/¼ cup) puffed quinoa

4 tablespoons Petal spice (page 55), plus an extra tablespoon for sprinkling

125 ml (4 fl oz/½ cup) olive oil

⅓ cup maple syrup

2 tablespoons rosewater

1 tablespoon vanilla bean paste

1 organic free-range egg white

85 g (3 oz/½ cup) dried cranberries

40 g (1½ oz/½ cup) dried blueberries

4 dried apple rings, coarsely torn

4 dried figs, roughly chopped

Preheat the oven to 170°C (340°F).

Combine the oats, nuts, coconut, quinoa and petal spice on a rimmed baking tray.

Drizzle the olive oil across the mixture, followed by the maple syrup, rosewater and vanilla. Use your hands to gently mix until everything is thoroughly coated. Drizzle the egg white over the mixture and toss again. Ensure the mixture is in an even layer and press down gently on the tray to flatten.

Bake for 30 minutes, then rotate the pan for even cooking, and bake for a further 15–20 minutes, or until the granola is beautifully golden, even dark golden in spots. If the mixture is taking on too much colour, you can cover it with foil then remove it for the last 20 minutes of cooking.

Remove the pan from the oven and immediately sprinkle the remaining tablespoon of petal spice over the top. Allow the granola to cool completely without stirring. Use a metal spatula to lift the granola from the pan and then stir the dried fruit through. Break the granola up enough to store in an airtight container for up to 2 weeks.

Note

- If you were particularly taken by this recipe and were subjected to the purchase of the world's largest bag of puffed quinoa (why the hell are they all so oversized?) never fear, try the Pear and quince crumble on page 241, or the Tahini yoghurt salmon with puffed grain dukkah on 187 to help you put a dint in that bag.

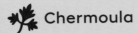 # Chermoula

 # Harissa

 # Olive tapenade

 # Zhug

Totally pasted

The following pastes, marinades and dips create generous flavours that are low on fuss. A rustic paste brimming with herbs, spices and fragrance will make simple dishes look and taste very, very good. It will seem like huge time and effort has been involved, when in fact it takes nothing more than a few turns in a blender to make meals that leave every plate cleared, licked clean and ready for seconds.

Chermoula

I don't have too many non-negotiables when cooking. People are mostly appalled by my slapdash approach, but one steadfast rule is the importance of dry-frying and grinding your spices. It's a crucial step that releases a bounty of oil (and flavour). It's the thing that will make this chermoula truly sing. The shelf life of this paste is a few weeks, so if you are uncertain how much you will use, opt for a smaller quantity.

To make 250 g	To make 500 g	To make 750 g
(9 oz/2 cups)	(1 lb 2 oz/4 cups)	(1 lb 11 oz/6 cups)
1 tbsp coriander seeds, toasted in a dry pan until fragrant	2 tbsp coriander seeds, toasted in a dry pan until fragrant	3 tbsp coriander seeds, toasted in a dry pan until fragrant
1 tbsp cumin seeds, toasted in a dry pan until fragrant	2 tbsp cumin seeds, toasted in a dry pan until fragrant	3 tbsp cumin seeds, toasted in a dry pan until fragrant
1 preserved lemon, or to taste	2 preserved lemons, or to taste	3 preserved lemons, or to taste
1 cup flat-leaf (Italian) parsley leaves	2 cups flat-leaf (Italian) parsley leaves	3 cups flat-leaf (Italian) parsley leaves
1 cup coriander (cilantro) leaves	2 cups coriander (cilantro) leaves	3 cups coriander (cilantro) leaves
375 ml (12½ fl oz/1½ cups) extra-virgin olive oil	750 ml (25½ fl oz/3 cups) extra-virgin olive oil	1.25 litres (42 fl oz/5 cups) extra-virgin olive oil
8 garlic cloves, peeled	16 garlic cloves, peeled	24 garlic cloves, peeled
2 tsp sumac	4 tsp sumac	2 tbsp sumac
4 tsp aleppo pepper	8 tsp aleppo pepper	4 tbsp aleppo pepper
2 tsp sweet smoked paprika	4 tsp sweet smoked paprika	2 tbsp sweet smoked paprika
2 tsp salt	4 tsp salt	2 tbsp salt
1 tsp turmeric	2 tsp turmeric	1 tbsp turmeric

Using a mortar and pestle, grind the coriander and cumin. (See above regarding non-negotiables.) Rinse the preserved lemon, then scrape off and discard the pulp. Transfer the peel to a blender or food processor with the remaining ingredients and blend until combined but still a little chunky.

Store in a jar in the fridge for a few weeks. You could stretch it further; I often have and everyone has lived to see another day.

Chermoula saganaki 'n' honey

If you can get your mitts on some smoked honey, it is life changing. Culinary purists will be aghast at my mashing of culinary cultures, but this is, quite simply, a must for flavour seekers. After a long day, eating this with a glass of wine is a legitimate dinner option. If you are pulling out all the stops, it also makes a spectacular addition to a table spread. **Serves 2–4 as a side**

2 slices of saganaki cheese (approx. 200 g/7 oz)

flour, for dredging

2 tablespoons olive oil

125 g (4½ oz/½ cup) Chermoula (page 67)

3 tablespoons smoked honey

squeeze of lemon juice

Dredge the slices of saganaki in flour, dusting off the excess.

Place a non-stick frying pan over medium-high heat. Add the olive oil and, once shimmering, add the saganaki, cooking until it has started to soften and taken on a glorious golden hue. Use a spatula and carefully flip – it will be soft so you need to ensure your spatula is squarely underneath it to take the load. Add the honey and cook for an additional minute before removing from the heat and, working quickly, plating the saganaki and topping with chermoula to taste. Season generously with salt and freshly ground black pepper and finish with a squeeze of lemon juice.

Best eaten piping hot with the danger of burning the roof of your mouth.

Chermoula kohlrabi and apple salad with smoked almonds and herbs

Have protein to grill. Make salad. Meal done. If only all weeknight dinners or random weekend lunches went this smoothly. **Serves 4–6 as part of a spread**

2 apples, shredded (don't be fussy, any on hand will do – red/green/ in between)

1 kohlrabi, peeled, sliced then julienned

juice and zest of 1 unwaxed lemon

80 g (2¾ oz/½ cup) smoked almonds, roughly chopped

½ cup coriander (cilantro) leaves, finely chopped

½ cup flat-leaf (Italian) parsley leaves, finely chopped

4 tablespoons Chermoula (page 67)

250 ml (8½ fl oz/1 cup) kewpie mayonnaise

Add the shredded apple and kohlrabi to a bowl. Add the lemon juice and zest and toss quickly to combine.

Combine the chermoula and mayonnaise in a bowl, then add to the kohlrabi and apple mixture. Stir to coat. Add the herbs and chopped almonds and another squeeze of lemon juice (if you have one floating) for freshness. Season with salt and freshly ground black pepper and serve.

Seeded chermoula salmon carpaccio

One of my favourite things to eat is salmon so fresh it could almost tell you where it was swimming yesterday. This dish takes moments to throw together but tastes like so much more. If/when I regain the energy to have another dinner party, this is the dish I will throw into the mix. The chermoula is done, and if you pre-roast the pepitas, it's a simple on-the-spot assembly. Winning. **Serves 2–4**

70 g (2½ oz/½ cup) pepitas
    (pumpkin seeds)

½ tablespoon olive oil

125 g (4½ oz/½ cup) Chermoula
    (page 67), plus an extra
    2 tablespoons

500 g (1 lb 2 oz) sashimi-grade
    salmon, sliced

coriander (cilantro) leaves,
    to scatter

Preheat the oven to 170°C (340°F).

Add the pepitas, olive oil and 2 tablespoons of the chermoula to a bowl and, using a spoon, stir to combine and ensure the pepitas are coated in the mixture. Spread across a large baking tray lined with baking paper. Pop in the oven and roast for 15 minutes. Remove and allow to cool.

Drizzle a serving platter with a splash of olive oil. Add the slices of salmon sashimi, then spoon over some extra chermoula. Scatter over the toasted pepitas. You don't need to use all the remaining chermoula, just dollop enough on so that every piece of salmon has a lovely hit of spice.

Scatter with the coriander and season with salt and freshly ground black pepper. Serve immediately with extra chermoula on the side.

Chermoula tomahawk and tomatoes

There is a lot of searing, blistering, smoking and flaming going on here. And I'm loving it. Summer toms are the perfect partner for the chermoula, adding sweetness and acidity to cut through the richness of the meat. Tomahawks can be expensive, so don't leave something this glorious to chance. Make sure you use a meat thermometer to get the right internal temperature. **Serves 4**

1 tomahawk steak (approx. 1 kg/ 2 lb 3 oz)

olive oil

185 g (6½ oz/¾ cup) Chermoula (page 67)

500 g (1 lb 2 oz) cherry tomatoes on the vine

brown sugar

Preheat your oven to 130°C (265°F).

Place the tomahawk in a roasting pan and add 1 tablespoon of olive oil. Cover with salt and freshly ground black pepper and smear just enough chermoula to cover both sides (roughly 4 tablespoons).

Pop the pan in the oven and cook for 40 minutes or as soon as the internal temperature hits 40°C (104°F) internal temperature. Check from 30 minutes – all oven heats vary.

Place the cherry tomatoes, an additional 60 g (2 oz/¼ cup) chermoula and a splash of olive oil in a roasting tin and cook in the oven for 25 minutes. The tomatoes will blister and begin to break down, creating the perfect sauce for your steak.

Preheat a barbecue grill plate to high. Sear the for a few minutes each side until you reach an internal temperature of 60°C and the chermoula has caramelised and charred.

Let the steak rest in a warm spot for 10 minutes.

While the steak is resting, remove the tomatoes from the oven. Season with salt, pepper and a pinch of brown sugar to temper the acidity. Add another tablespoon of chermoula and stir to combine. They should be caramelised and there should be quite a bit of juice in your pan.

To serve, place the steak on a large board or platter. Spoon over the tomatoes and their juices. Season with salt and pepper and serve with extra chermoula on the side.

Caramelised leek, chermoula and chickpea dip dinner

There is nothing better than a meal you can swipe through with soft bread. This is a condiment-salad-dressing-sauce situation; organised mayhem held together by chermoula-addled hummus and Big Dip Energy. Fire-licked in all the right places; it's an absolute winner. You can prepare the hummus ahead of time and store in the fridge; just try not to eat it all before you make this. **Serves 4 as part of a spread**

120 ml (4 fl oz) olive oil, plus extra to drizzle

3 leeks, white part only, washed and sliced into thin rings

½ white onion, diced

2 garlic cloves

1 teaspoon each cumin and coriander seeds, lightly crushed

400 g (14 oz) tinned diced tomatoes

4 tablespoons Chermoula (page 67), plus extra to serve

400 g (14 oz) tinned chickpeas, thoroughly rinsed and drained

3 tablespoons each mint and coriander (cilantro), thinly sliced

flatbreads, to serve

coriander (cilantro) sprigs, to serve

Chermoula hummus

2 tablespoons chermoula

400 g (14 oz) tinned chickpeas, thoroughly rinsed and drained

1 garlic clove

juice and zest of ½ unwaxed lemon

2 tablespoons hulled tahini

2 tablespoons iced water (you may need more depending on thickness of hummus)

Make the hummus by adding all the ingredients to a food processor and blitzing until smooth and creamy. If your hummus seems too thick and grainy, add more iced water, 1 tablespoon at a time, until the desired consistency is achieved. Season with salt and freshly ground black pepper.

Add 4 tablespoons of the olive oil to a frying pan over low heat. Add the leeks and a generous pinch of salt. Cook, stirring regularly, until the leeks are soft and caramelised with a few lovely bits of fired char here and there, up to 25 minutes.

While the leeks are cooking, place another frying pan over medium–low heat. Once hot, add the remaining olive oil. Add the diced onion and cook, stirring regularly, for 5–8 minutes or until soft and translucent. Add the garlic and cumin and coriander seeds and cook for another minute. Add the diced tomatoes, chermoula and chickpeas and simmer for 20 minutes. Add the leeks, stir gently to incorporate and cook until warmed through.

Add the hummus to a serving plate. Drizzle with olive oil and season with salt and pepper. Add the chickpea chermoula mixture to the centre, scatter with a few coriander sprigs. Serve with additional chermoula and flatbreads for swiping.

Time-saving hacks

- Use store-bought hummus.
- Tinned chickpeas are always fine. Honestly, if you have the forethought to soak, I commend you. For the rest of us – grab thy tin with pride.

Chermoula and haloumi lamb meatballs with lemon

Sometimes you just can't beat a bit of meat and sauce. The chermoula and lemon give this such a glorious unexpected and bright twist. It does need a bit of time on the stove, so it's a cook-it-on-the-weekend to eat-sometime-during-the-week kinda meal. It also does marvellously well for a double-batch-and-freeze scenario. **Serves 6**

4 slices white bread, crusts removed

250 ml (8½ fl oz/1 cup) milk

500 g (1 lb 2 oz) minced (ground) lamb

1 small onion, peeled and diced

4 tablespoons Chermoula (page 67)

1 × 200 g (7 oz) block haloumi, grated

¾ cup chopped flat-leaf (Italian) parsley, plus extra to serve

2 garlic cloves, crushed

1 large organic free-range egg, lightly beaten

extra-virgin olive oil, for frying

coriander (cilantro) sprigs, to serve

Sauce

3 tablespoons olive oil

2 onions, finely diced

3 tablespoons Chermoula

5 garlic cloves, crushed

800 g (1 lb 12 oz) tinned crushed tomatoes

1 lemon, thinly sliced

60 g (2 oz/¼ cup) tomato paste (concentrated purée)

2 teaspoons brown sugar

500 ml (17 fl oz/2 cups) chicken stock

Make the meatballs by soaking the bread in the milk until soft. Squeeze the bread to remove any residual milk. Add the soft bread to a large bowl with the beef, onion, chermoula, haloumi, parsley, garlic and egg. Season with salt and freshly ground black pepper, then get your hands in there. Massage the ingredients until fully incorporated. Roll the mixture into golf ball-sized meatballs and set aside on a tray until you have rolled all of the beef mixture.

In a heavy-based large frying pan or saucepan, heat the olive oil over medium heat and, working in batches, sear the meatballs all over until golden, about 5 minutes. Gently remove from the pan and set aside.

Make the sauce in the same pan by adding the olive oil. Once hot, sauté the onions until soft and translucent. Add the chermoula and garlic and cook for another 1–2 minutes. Add the tomatoes, lemon, tomato paste and brown sugar and give everything a really good stir. Add the stock and simmer for 10–15 minutes or until the sauce has begun to thicken and reduce slightly. Place the seared meatballs in the sauce and continue to cook for 40 minutes or until the sauce has thickened and the flavours have intensified. Taste and season with salt and pepper.

Scatter with the coriander when ready to serve.

Harissa

Harissa is so full of flavour, one spoonful will slap you around the chops, then slap you again just to be sure. It's not only the heat but the smokiness and the bitter hint of lemon that make it such a zinging marvel. Have a fresh pot in your fridge and you'll transform all manner of dishes, from a dollop on poached eggs, spread across your avo toast, or slathered on bits 'n' bobs of veg found in the back of the crisper and roasted. The addition of Mexican chillies to a north African condiment may seem strange, but I learnt this trick from a Californian restaurant and never looked back. It adds so much smoky depth, and while non-traditional – this is more a chilli-based sauce with north African spices – it gives it a distinctive and addictive flavour.

To make 280 g
(10 oz/1 cup)

7 dried guajillo chillies

1 red chilli, chopped

125 ml (4 fl oz/½ cup) grapeseed oil (or other flavourless oil)

2 garlic cloves

1½ tbsp each cumin seeds and coriander seeds, toasted in a dry pan until fragrant, roughly ground

¼ preserved lemon, pith removed, skin diced

2 tsp sweet smoked paprika

2 tsp tomato paste (concentrated purée)

pinch of sugar

pinch of caraway seeds

To make 560 g
(1 lb 4 oz/2 cups)

15 dried guajillo chillies

2 red chillies, chopped

250 ml (8½ fl oz/1 cup) grapeseed oil (or other flavourless oil)

4 garlic cloves

3 tbsp each cumin seeds and coriander seeds, toasted in a dry pan until fragrant, roughly ground

½ preserved lemon, pith removed, skin diced

4 tsp sweet smoked paprika

4 tsp tomato paste (concentrated purée)

pinch of sugar

1 tsp caraway seeds

To make 1.12 kg
(2.5 lb 7 oz/4 cups)

30 dried guajillo chillies

4 red chillies, chopped

500 ml (17 fl oz/2 cups) grapeseed oil (or other flavourless oil)

8 garlic cloves

120 ml (4 fl oz) olive oil

¼ cup (2 oz) each cumin seeds and coriander seeds, toasted in a dry pan until fragrant, roughly ground

1 preserved lemon, pith removed, skin diced

1 tbsp sweet smoked paprika

1 tbsp tomato paste (concentrated purée)

2 tsp sugar

2 tsp caraway seeds

Bring a large pot of water to the boil. Add the dried chillies, reduce the heat to medium–low and gently simmer to rehydrate the chillies, about 20 minutes. Drain then, when cool enough to handle, remove and discard the stems. Make sure to drain any water that may be trapped inside the chillies.

Add the chillies with the remining ingredients to a blender and blitz until you get a smooth paste. The oil will eventually separate a little when this settles but I love that. If you want a really spreadable harissa, blitz for a little longer and add a tablespoon or two of water – this will emulsify it and make it a little creamier in texture.

Will keep for up to 3 months in a tightly sealed jar in the fridge.

Harissa maple-roasted pumpkin with haloumi and burghul salad

This is game-changing salad. 1. Good on its own. 2. Good after a long gestation in the back of the fridge and 3. Marvellous served alongside all manner of grilled proteins. Given how time-poor we all are, I feel like this is the trifecta every salad must meet. To keep this vegan, you could replace the haloumi with a good cashew cheese. If you have a batch of Ultimate ranch dressing (see page 201) at the ready, simply sub that for the herb-blitzed yoghurt in this recipe. Both work a treat. **Serves 4**

3 tablespoons olive oil

600 g (1 lb 5 oz) Japanese or Kent pumpkin (winter squash), deseeded and cut into large chunks

3 tablespoons maple syrup

4–6 tablespoons Harissa (page 78)

175 g (6 oz/1 cup) burghul (bulgur wheat)

375 ml (12½ fl oz/1½ cups) vegetable stock

250 g (9 oz/1 cup) Greek yoghurt

½ cup coarsely torn mint leaves

½ cup basil leaves

1 tablespoon olive oil

3–4 slices haloumi

To serve

1–2 tablespoons Harissa per serve

3 tablespoons pepitas (pumpkin seeds) per serve

Preheat the oven to 165°C (330°F).

Drizzle a little olive oil on a large flat baking tray, then place the pumpkin on the tray. Combine the remaining olive oil, maple syrup and harissa in a bowl, then smear the mixture all over the pumpkin, using your hands.

Season generously with salt and freshly ground black pepper, pop in the oven to roast until caramelised and cooked through. This can take between 25–40 minutes depending on the size of your pumpkin pieces.

Put the burghul in a bowl. Bring the stock to the boil, then pour it over the burghul until just covered. Set aside for 10 minutes for the stock to absorb and use a fork to stir a few times to fluff the grains. I always like to be a little generous with the stock as the absorption rate can vary between batches of burghul and there is nothing more frustrating than realising your stock has been completely absorbed by the burghul before it has finished softening. (You can reserve any leftover stock for another use.) Set aside to cool, then stir through the mint. Season with salt and freshly ground pepper.

Add the yoghurt, mint and basil to a blender and blitz to combine. Season with salt and pepper.

Place a small non-stick frying pan over medium heat and, once warm, add 1 tablespoon of olive oil and the haloumi. Cook until lightly golden on one side, 1–2 minutes, then flip to cook the other side.

Smear the herb yoghurt across the base of a serving plate. Top with torn pieces of grilled haloumi and your pumpkin pieces. Scoop the burghul on top, then drizzle with the harissa. Scatter with pepitas, give another generous season with salt and pepper and serve.

Pasta with kale sauce and harissa

There are only so many pesto pastas we can consume in a lifetime, but this kale version adapted from chef Joshua McFadden is a lighter option, and the ultimate passenger for the harissa. I love the epic colour contrast and it's one of the best quick dinner options around. There are no hard 'n' fast rules – think of it like a cocktail mixing in the blender - add a bit, taste a bit, add a bit more. I like my flavours dialled up to 11, but if you want a more mellow dish then ditch the preserved lemon. **Serves 3**

500–600 g (1 lb 2 oz–1 lb 5 oz) fresh tagliatelle or fettuccine

grated parmesan, plus extra to serve

olive oil, to drizzle

140 g (5 oz/½ cup) Harissa (page 78)

Kale sauce

3 garlic cloves

60 ml (2 fl oz/¼ cup) olive oil

500 g (1 lb 2 oz) cavolo nero (Tuscan kale), stems stripped, leaves roughly chopped

¼ preserved lemon, flesh removed, skin sliced (you only use the skin)

75 g (¾ cup) parmesan, grated

For the kale sauce, bring a large pot of generously salted water to the boil.

Add the garlic and olive oil to a small heavy-based pot over medium heat and cook until the garlic begins to sizzle. Reduce the heat to low and cook until the garlic is light golden, soft and fragrant. Allow to cool, then pour the oil and garlic into a blender.

When the water is boiling, add the kale leaves and boil until they are tender but not overcooked, about 5 minutes. Pull them out with tongs or a slotted spoon and transfer them to the blender with a splosh of the cooking water. Add the preserved lemon. Blitz. Allow to cool slightly, then add half the parmesan and blitz again. If you add the parmesan too early it will clump together because the heat of the kale and water will cause it to soften and melt. Blitz until you achieve a smooth, vibrant green sauce.

Add the pasta to the still-boiling water and cook until al dente. With a ladle or measuring cup, scoop out about a cup of the pasta water and reserve, then drain the pasta.

Transfer the drained pasta back to the pot and pour in the kale purée. Add the remaining parmesan and toss well. Add a touch more pasta water and toss until the pasta noodles are well coated with the bright green sauce. Alternatively, you can sit the pasta on top of the vibrant sauce like I have done here. Serve right away with a big drizzle of olive oil and harissa. Scatter with extra parmesan if you think it needs it.

Roasted beetroot with whipped feta, harissa, coriander seeds and honey

This is almost too pretty to eat. Almost. The sweet, earthy flavour of the beetroot is brilliantly matched with the harissa. You can serve this as a cold salad (oh hey, 'bring-a-plate', I see you) or with the beetroot still warm from roasting. **Serves 2–4**

½ small bunch each red, yellow and Chioggia beetroot (beets), leafy tops removed, well-scrubbed

3 tablespoons red wine vinegar

1 tablespoon olive oil

3 tablespoons lightly crushed coriander seeds

3 tablespoons honey

2–4 tablespoons Harissa (page 78), to drizzle

Whipped feta

75 g (2¾ oz/½ cup) crumbled Persian feta

250 g (9 oz) crème fraîche

60 g (2 oz/¼ cup) plain yoghurt

1 garlic clove, crushed

Preheat the oven to 170°C (340°F).

Place the beetroot in a roasting dish. Combine the vinegar, olive oil, coriander seeds and honey in a bowl and stir to combine. Pour the mixture over the beetroot and toss to combine. Cover tightly with foil and pop in the oven to cook for about 40 minutes or until the beetroot can be pierced easily with a knife. Remove the foil and cook for another 1–2 minutes until all the liquid has mostly evaporated and the beetroots are glossy. Leave in the dish to cool while you prepare the whipped feta.

Add the whipped feta ingredients to a blender and blitz until smooth and creamy, about 30 seconds. Spread the mixture over the base of a serving plate. Halve some of the beetroots, then add them and any remaining pan juices and spices from the roasting dish over the whipped feta. Drizzle with the harissa to taste, season with salt and freshly ground black pepper and serve.

Orange, harissa and olive salad

Fruit in salads. Divisive I know. But I like living on the edge – it feels thrilling, simple and optimistic. Just like this salad. **Serves 4–6**

6 oranges, peeled, pith removed and flesh chopped in whatever way you see fit

80 g (2¾ oz/½ cup) pitted dried olives

3 tablespoons Harissa (page 78), or more to taste

75 g (2¾ oz/½ cup) crumbled Persian feta

½ cup coriander (cilantro) leaves, chopped

a few coriander flowers, if you happen to feel fancy

Add the chopped oranges, olives and harissa to a bowl. Toss gently to coat the orange in the harissa mixture and set aside for 15 minutes – the juice is just going to explode during this time. Add the remaining ingredients and toss gently again to combine. The harissa and juice work like a dressing – it's magical. Taste and adjust the seasoning and add more harissa if you are seeking more heat. Scatter with those fancy-feeling coriander flowers and serve.

Olive tapenade

Rid your mind of the 'café style' toasted Turkish bread sandwiches spread with olive tapenade popularised in the noughties and '90s. This is one of the most undervalued condiments to have in your repertoire, and it's ready for a comeback. Salty, briny, with a whisper of smoke, its applications are many and varied from a cheese platter to sides and stand-alone meals. Keep this vegetarian by omitting the anchovies and replace with ½ tablespoon nutritional yeast flakes for every anchovy.

To make 220 g
(8 oz/1 cup)

1½ cups soft herbs (I used a mix of flat-leaf/Italian parsley, dill and a few random basil leaves)

155 g (5½ oz/1 cup) pitted kalamata olives

3 cloves smoked garlic

1 tbsp capers

2 anchovies

juice and zest of ½ large unwaxed lemon

pinch of urfa biber or red chilli flakes

75 ml (2½ fl oz) olive oil plus more to cover leftovers

To make 440 g
(15½ oz/2 cups)

3 cups soft herbs

310 g (11 oz/2 cups) pitted kalamata olives

6 cloves smoked garlic

2 tbsp capers

4 anchovies

juice and zest of 1 large unwaxed lemon

½ tbsp urfa biber or red chilli flakes

150 ml (5 fl oz) olive oil plus more to cover leftovers

To make 880 g
(1 lb 15 oz/4 cups)

6 cups soft herbs

620 g (1 lb 6 oz/4 cups) pitted kalamata olives

12 cloves smoked garlic

4 tbsp capers

8 anchovies

juice and zest of 2 large unwaxed lemons

1 tbsp urfa biber or red chilli flakes

300 ml (10 fl oz) olive oil plus more to cover leftovers

Add the ingredients to a chopper or blender and blitz until a paste-like consistency is achieved. Scrape down the sides and blitz again. If it seems too thick just add extra olive oil. Store in an airtight container with a film of oil to prevent it from drying out in the fridge. This will keep in the fridge for up to 3 months in a tightly sealed jar.

Roasted taters with olive tapenade and horseradish cream

This is one of the dishes I crave most. Salty, crisp, and hot in both temperature and taste, it's the ultimate sensory and gustatory overload. It does well at a fancy brunch as well as placating any feelings that may come the day after the (big) night before. **Serves 4–6 as part of a spread**

1 kg (2 lb 3 oz) floury, medium-starch potatoes

185 ml (6 fl oz/¾ cup) olive oil

1 tablespoon (minimum) fresh horseradish, or to taste

125–185 g (4–6 fl oz/½–¾ cup) crème fraîche

110 g (4 oz/½ cup) Olive tapenade (page 89), or to taste

Preheat the oven to 200°C (390°F).

Parboil the potatoes in a large pot of boiling water. Squish them with a fork in a roasting tin. This helps them absorb the oil and crisp delightfully as you cook them. Generously douse in oil like you are trying to put out a fire, then pop the potatoes in the oven until amazing gnarly crispy bits start to emerge – probably around the 25 minute mark.

While the potatoes are cooking, use a Microplane to grate the fresh horseradish into the crème fraîche. Smear this over the base of a serving plate. Top with your crispy goodness, then top with spoonfulls of the olive tapenade. Serve nice 'n' hot.

Olive tapenade

Quick 'n' dirty olive pasta with prosciutto, spinach and olives

This is how you feed a crowd. The unannounced type. The best type, because it means family or good friends – the only ones to drop in on a whim, hang around and decide to stay for dinner. It's also the dish I turn to most when I just need to get dinner done. When all the wheels are off, people are hungry, and 'being fed' is the order of the day; you'll have this on the table in the time it takes to cook the pasta. **Serves 4**

250 g (9 oz) dried spaghetti

165–220 g (6–8 oz/¾–1 cup) Olive tapenade (page 89), or to taste

1 tablespoon olive oil, plus extra to serve

2 cups English spinach (optional)

80 g (2¾ oz) prosciutto, coarsely torn

70 g (2½ oz/½ cup) pitted wild olives

50 g (1¾ oz/½ cup) shaved parmesan

juice of 1 lemon

Cook the pasta in a large pot of salted boiling water until al dente. Strain quickly and return to the pan. Add the olive tapenade and olive oil and toss to coat the pasta. Add the spinach and season generously with salt and freshly ground black pepper. Add the prosciutto, olives and parmesan and toss to combine. Season again with salt, pepper and lemon juice. Taste and adjust the seasoning. Squeeze over some more lemon juice for brightness if needed.

Using tongs, transfer the pasta to serving bowls. Drizzle with a little extra olive oil (optional) and more olive tapenade to taste, and serve while still nice and hot.

Olive tapenade

Nectarine, burrata, olive tapenade and basil salad

Welcome to the world's quickest salad. When stone fruits are in their peak, this is an Italian summer holiday on a plate. If you have a super-sweet leaning, substitute the slightly tart yellow nectarines with white ones, as they tend to be more saccharine. **Serves 4**

1–2 burrata balls (approx. 200 g/ 7 oz each) or buffalo mozzarella if unavailable

6 yellow nectarines, stones removed, cut into wedges

110 g (4 oz/½ cup) Olive tapenade (page 89)

baby basil leaves, to scatter

2–3 tablespoons extra-virgin olive oil

Tear the burrata into large pieces, place in serving bowls and scatter the nectarine wedges over the top. Add 1 tablespoon of tapenade to each plate, dolloping wherever you like. Scatter the basil leaves over and add a generous glug of olive oil. Season generously with salt and freshly ground black pepper and serve.

Olive tapenade

Shallot, olive tapenade and date roast chicken

Another multitasker. This is like a mum in dinner form. She throws her weight around midweek, is perfect special-occasion fodder should the moment require it, and is prepare-ahead enough to pull off for a dinner party. **Serves 4**

2 tablespoons olive oil

15 g (½ oz) unsalted butter

4 organic free-range chicken leg quarters, bone in, skin on, at room temperature

10 small French shallots, peeled

4 garlic cloves, whole

185 ml (6 fl oz/¾ cup) white wine

10 sprigs lemon thyme, plus a few extra leaves to serve

110 g (4 oz/½ cup) Olive tapenade (page 89)

375 ml (12½ fl oz/1½ cups) chicken stock

8 medjool dates, pitted and halved

zest and juice of 1 unwaxed lemon

Preheat the oven to 200°C (390°F).

Generously season the chicken with salt and freshly ground black pepper.

Place a cast-iron pan or ovenproof frying pan over medium heat. Once hot, add the olive oil and butter. Once shimmering and the butter has melted, add the chicken, skin side down. You might like to place a plate over the chicken to weight it down and to help maximise the browning of the skin. Cook until the skin is crispy and golden, about 4 minutes. Remove the chicken from the pan.

Add the shallots and garlic cloves to the liquid in the pan and cook over low heat, undisturbed, until caramelised and golden, giving the pan the odd shake to turn them as they cook. Continue to cook until they look quite soft. Deglaze the pan with the wine and cook until reduced by half. Add the lemon thyme sprigs, 2 tablespoons of the olive tapenade and the stock to the pan. Simmer until slightly reduced. Season with salt and pepper and add the dates to the sauce. Return the chicken to the pan, skin side up, and place in the oven. Roast until the chicken is just cooked through, about 20 minutes.

Dollop the remaining olive tapenade over the top and give it a moment to warm in the residual heat of the pan.

Squeeze the lemon juice over the top and scatter with the zest and a few additional lemon thyme leaves. Season with salt and pepper and transfer to serving plates, scooping up the glorious sweet and salty reduced sauce.

Ultimate savoury French toast

This is loosely based on Hong Kong-style French toast, but I wanted a savoury version. I find sweeter versions just a little cloying, but the salty elements really cut through the richness here for breakfast, brunch, lunch, dunch (dinner-lunch) magic. This is merely a guide – you can layer as many slices of bread and fillings as you see fit. This recipe allows enough batter for two sandwiches, so double the quantity if you decide to do multilayered sandwiches. **Serves 1**

2–4 slices bread per serve

1 tablespoon Olive tapenade (page 89) per layer

1 tablespoon crumbled Persian feta per layer

2 teaspoons spicy tomato relish (or use Bloody useful red sauce on page 124) per layer

grapeseed oil, for frying

1 organic free-range egg per serve

dill fronds, to finish

Batter

2 large organic free-range eggs

60 ml (2 fl oz/¼ cup) pouring (single/light) cream

60 ml (2 fl oz/¼ cup) milk

Preheat the oven to 180°C (360°F).

Whisk the batter ingredients in a bowl until incorporated, then set aside.

Layer your sandwich by spreading each condiment and the Persian feta on the same slice of bread in layers. Top with another piece of bread. Repeat, depending on how many layers you want to achieve.

Gently transfer the loaded sandwich to the batter. Let it have a good sitz bath, 5 minutes each side, carefully turning with a pair of tongs and a spatula. Also make sure the sides are covered/soaked in batter.

Place a deep-sided non-stick frying pan over medium heat. Add enough oil to generously coat the base of the pan. Once hot and shimmering, gently lower the sandwich into the oil. Cook for 45 seconds each side or until golden. You need to watch this closely, so it doesn't burn, using the same spatula and tongs to turn the sandwich in the hot oil. Drain on paper towel. Immediately transfer to a lined baking tray and pop in the oven to keep warm while you cook the eggs.

Place another non-stick frying pan over medium heat and add a cracked egg and cook for approximately 2 minutes for a soft yolk.

Transfer the sandwich to a plate. Top with the egg and scatter with dill fronds. Season generously with salt and freshly ground black pepper and serve.

Risotto with nduja, stracciatella and olive tapenade

Some reality cooking shows declare it the 'dish of death', but there is no greater comfort than a bowl of beautifully made risotto. This recipe is just so lovely – the spicy nduja and briny olive tapenade contrasting with the creamy stracciatella and the bitey mouthfeel of the rice. I imagine this eaten by the fire, with an open bottle of red, either completely solitary or surrounded by the finest of company. Just don't skip on finishing with the entirely necessary *mantecatura* – a final lashing of butter and cheese – which gives risotto its luscious richness. **Serves 4–6**

80 ml (2½ fl oz/⅓ cup) olive oil

1 white onion, finely diced

2 garlic cloves, grated

1 tablespoon salt

70 g (2½ oz) nduja spreadable sausage

440 g (15½ oz/2 cups) carnoli rice (or arborio)

80 g (2¾ oz/½ cup) pitted smoked kalamata olives, sliced

250 ml (8½ fl oz/1 cup) dry white wine

750 ml (25½ fl oz/3 cups) chicken stock (with an additional cup of stock in reserve), warmed on the stove

2 tablespoons stracciatella

40 g (1½ oz) unsalted butter, cubed

To serve

4–6 tablespoons Olive tapenade (page 89)

4–6 tablespoons stracciatella

2 tablespoons finely chopped flat-leaf (Italian) parsley

Heat the oil in a wide casserole dish over medium–low heat. Add the onion and garlic and stir until soft, 8–10 minutes. Season with salt and add the nduja, stirring constantly to prevent catching. Cook until the sausage has released its oils and the onion mixture has taken on a glorious muddy red tinge.

Add the rice, stirring constantly – you want to coat the grains in the oily mixture and also toast them, at least 1 minute. Add the olives, stirring to incorporate, then add the wine and cook until almost completely evaporated, 2–3 minutes. Add the hot stock, one ladleful at a time, stirring continuously until absorbed before adding another. The constant stirring serves to transform the rice's soft starch into a clinging agent, binding the grains together. The amount of stock required will vary according to the type of rice and evaporation so have extra on hand in case.

Cook until the rice is al dente, 20–25 minutes, then remove from the heat and let stand for 1 minute. Beat in the butter and stracciatella until combined and creamy. Season to taste and serve immediately by scooping the risotto into serving bowls. Top with 1 tablespoon of olive tapenade per serve and 1 tablespoon of stracciatella. I often spill some at this point, adding a fair whack more – accidents happen after all. Season with salt and freshly ground black pepper, scatter with the parsley and serve.

Zhug

Zhug is a hot chilli sauce that originated in Yemen, sometimes spelled zhoug. It always asserts its presence but doesn't overtake, making it a useful marinade or paste-like dressing to have in your repertoire. That aside, it's just lovely to eat; fresh and curiously purifying amid all the herbaceous ingredients. And most importantly, it will help you deliver on your heat-bubbled promise of a decent dinner every single time.

To make 250 ml	To make 750 ml	To make 1.5 litres
(8½ fl oz/1 cup)	(25½ fl oz/3 cups)	(51 fl oz/6 cups)
¾ tbsp coriander seeds	2 tbsp coriander seeds	4 tbsp coriander seeds
¾ tbsp cumin seeds	2 tbsp cumin seeds	4 tbsp cumin seeds
small pinch of caraway seeds	½ tsp caraway seeds	1 tsp caraway seeds
125 ml (4 fl oz/½ cup) grapeseed oil	375 ml (12½ fl oz/1½ cups) grapeseed oil	750 ml (25½ fl oz/3 cups) grapeseed oil
¾ bunch flat-leaf (Italian) parsley, thick stems removed	2 bunches flat-leaf (Italian) parsley, thick stems removed	4 bunches flat-leaf (Italian) parsley, thick stems removed
¼ bunch coriander (cilantro) leaves, roots and stems, rinsed	1 bunch coriander (cilantro), leaves, roots and stems, rinsed	2 bunches coriander (cilantro), leaves, roots, stems, rinsed
2½ green chillies	5 green chillies	10 green chillies
1 garlic clove, peeled	3 garlic cloves, peeled	6 garlic cloves
1½ tsp ground turmeric	2 tsp ground turmeric	1 tbsp ground turmeric
pinch of salt flakes	2 tsp salt flakes	1 tbsp salt flakes

Place a frying pan over low heat. Add the coriander seeds, cumin seeds and caraway seeds and toast, stirring constantly until fragrant. Remove from the heat and allow to cool before adding them to a spice grinder or mortar and pestle and grinding to a powder. Transfer to a blender and add the remaining ingredients, except the salt. Blitz until it just comes together. Season generously with salt. Store in a screw top jar in the fridge for up to a month.

Loaded honey and zhug roasted pumpkin

Fact: slow-roasted pumpkin is an edible pillow. Soft, comforting, supportive and yielding in spots. My love for it is strong and unending. Here it is in all its glory, laden with zhug, which just gives her glorious lift and oomph. This is a 'throw it all on the plate and serve' show-stopper. **Serves 3–4, or 6 as part of a spread**

1 heirloom butternut pumpkin (squash), cut in half lengthways, seeds removed

2 tablespoons olive oil

1 tablespoon honey

4 tablespoons Zhug (page 101), plus extra to serve

4–6 tablespoons labne

shredded kale leaves, to scatter

3 tablespoons cranberries

mint and coriander (cilantro) leaves, to scatter

40 g (1½ oz/¼ cup) smoked almonds, roughly chopped

2 tablespoons pine nuts

lemon juice, to season

Preheat the oven to 180°C (360°F).

Place a large frying pan over medium heat. Add the olive oil and, once shimmering, char the pumpkin, flesh down, until dark but not burnt, about 3 minutes. You will need to do this with each half.

Place the charred pumpkin, flesh side up, on a large baking tray lined with baking paper. Drizzle with the olive oil and rub with the honey. Roast for 30–45 minutes or until cooked through.

Gently transfer the pumpkin to a serving plate and drizzle with the zhug. Add the labne to the centre of the pumpkin along with the kale, cranberries, herbs and nuts. Season generously with lemon juice, salt and freshly ground black pepper and serve with extra zhug on the side.

Zhug

Spicy zhug chicken pie

The ultimate pie for your pie hole. I love chicken pie. And this zhug-hugged chicken is like a best friend. With pastry. **Serves 8**

3 tablespoons olive oil

1 kg (2 lb 3 oz) boneless, skinless chicken thighs

30 g (1 oz) unsalted butter

1 onion, finely diced

1 leek, white and pale green parts only, cut in half lengthways and thinly sliced

35 g (1¼ oz/¼ cup) plain (all-purpose) flour

250 ml (8½ fl oz/1 cup) chicken stock

185 ml (6 fl oz/¾ cup) milk

60 ml (2 fl oz/¼ cup) pouring (single/light) cream

185 ml (6 fl oz/¾ cup) Zhug (page 101) (or more depending on the heat intensity you like)

Pie pastry base

300 g (10½ oz/2 cups) plain (all-purpose) flour

5 g (⅛ oz) salt

150 g (5½ oz) unsalted butter

1½ teaspoons vinegar

80 ml (2½ fl oz/⅓ cup) iced water

To top

170 g (6 oz) puff pastry (approximately half a 320 g/ 11½ oz sheet)

1 organic free-range egg whisked with 1 tablespoon pouring (single/light) cream, for egg wash

2 teaspoons za'atar

For the pie pastry base, add the flour and salt to a bowl. Add the butter and, using your fingertips, rub the butter into the flour to partly combine. Combine the vinegar and iced water and sprinkle it over the flour mixture. Use the palm of your hand to knead the dough. You want to incorporate the ingredients but not overmix the dough so much that you completely blend the butter. The aim is to have streaks of marbled butter through the pastry – this will help to give a slightly flaky texture to the pie. Shape the dough into a disc about 2 cm (¾ in) thick, wrap in plastic wrap and refrigerate for 2 hours.

Place a frying pan over medium heat. Add 1 tablespoon of the olive oil and, once hot, add the chicken in batches and cook until brown and crisp and the meat has just cooked through. Transfer to a bowl and, while still warm, immediately shred the meat using two forks.

Melt the butter in a large heavy saucepan over medium heat. Add the remaining olive oil, onion and leek and sauté for 5 minutes or until just tender but not browned. Add the flour and immediately turn the heat to low, stirring constantly for 2 minutes. Slowly whisk in the chicken stock, milk and cream. Simmer for 5 minutes or until the sauce thickens. Stir in the shredded chicken and the zhug, adapting the quantity of zhug to taste. Season generously with salt and freshly ground black pepper and allow to cool.

Bring the dough to room temperature (about 20 minutes), then roll it out to a 4 mm (¼ in) thick round.

Preheat the oven to 180°C (360°F). Grease, then line a 25–28 cm (10–11 in) non-stick pie dish with pastry base dough, pressing it well into the sides with a slight overhang. Fill with the zhug chicken mixture. Brush the edge of the pastry with some of the egg wash, then layer over the puff pastry, pressing down around the edges to seal.

Pierce a hole in the centre to allow the steam to escape and brush the top of the pie with the remaining egg wash and scatter over the za'atar. Bake until the pie is deep golden, the pastry is cooked through and the filling is hot, 40–50 minutes.

Zhug slurpy mussels with parmesan fries

Quick, fast, fresh and delicious. You can't stuff it up. If only life was as easy as this recipe. It's one of my favourite ways to enjoy a slurpy bowl of clams. Serve in bowls designed for slurping and ensure everyone is supplied with a spoon. Best enjoyed in the sunshine with wine and friends. **Serves 4**

60 g (2 oz) salted butter

1 small onion, finely diced

2 garlic cloves, minced

60 ml (2 fl oz/¼ cup) Zhug (page 101), plus extra to serve

375 ml (12½ fl oz/1½ cups) white wine

1 × 400 ml (13½ fl oz) tin coconut milk

1.2 kg (2 lb 10 oz) mussels, debearded and scrubbed clean

Parmesan fries

4 all-purpose potatoes, peeled and cut into thick matchsticks

60–125 ml (2–4 fl oz/¼–½ cup) extra-virgin olive oil

1 tablespoon flaky sea salt

50 g (1¾ oz/½ cup) finely grated parmesan (with a Microplane), plus extra to serve

Preheat the oven to 210°C (410°F).

To make the parmesan fries, toss the potatoes with the olive oil and sea salt, then spread them out on a large baking tray lined with baking paper in a single layer. Bake for 20–25 minutes. Reduce the oven temperature to 200°C (390°F), turn the chips and bake for another 15 minutes. While still piping hot, grate over the parmesan using a Microplane.

While the chips are roasting, place a large saucepan over medium heat and add the butter. When the butter has melted and is just foaming, add the onion and cook until caramelised and soft, about 8 minutes. Add the garlic and cook until fragrant, then add the zhug. Stir to coat, then gently pour in the wine and coconut milk.

Increase the heat to high and bring to the boil. Add the mussels. Cover and cook, shaking the pan every few minutes or so, until the mussels have opened, about 5–8 minutes. Discard any unopened mussels. Tip into a large serving bowl and season with salt and freshly ground black pepper.

Remove the fries from the oven and toss with extra parmesan. Serve the mussels with the fries, all piping hot, with a little extra zhug dolloped over.

Tomato party

I live for tomatoes. In summer I am constantly seeking and eating them. Here they play together in all their forms – the pop of fresh, the collapsing roasted, and the smoky sweet chewiness of the semi-dried smoked versions. The slathering of feta and fragrant hit of zhug make this salad the life of any party. When showcasing a few ingredients like this there is nowhere to hide, so buy the best that you can find and afford. **Serves 2–4**

Roasting

450 g (1 lb/3 cups) cherry tomatoes

6–8 smoked garlic cloves

3 tablespoons olive oil

½ teaspoon cumin seeds, toasted in a dry pan until fragrant, then roughly ground

½ teaspoon coriander seeds, toasted in a dry pan until fragrant, then roughly ground

1 tablespoon honey

Dressing

60 ml (2 fl oz/¼ cup) Zhug (page 101)

1 teaspoon honey

½ teaspoon red wine vinegar

3 tablespoons extra-virgin olive oil

Salad

3 cups cherry tomatoes, halved

150 g (5½ oz/1 cup) smoked semi-dried tomatoes (the absolute best you can find), chopped

½ small red onion, finely diced

75 g (2¾ oz/½ cup) crumbled Persian feta

generous handful of basil leaves

Preheat the oven to 150°C (300°F).

Add the roasting ingredients to a baking dish and, using your hands, give everything a good toss. Roast until the tomatoes are blistered, soft and caramelised. This usually takes about an hour over the lower heat. Allow to cool, then peel the garlic cloves. Transfer half of the cloves to a bowl and use a fork to gently crush them.

To the same bowl, add all the dressing ingredients, except for the olive oil, and whisk to combine. Continue whisking and slowly stream in the olive oil until the dressing is smooth and emulsified. Adjust the seasoning with salt and freshly ground black pepper.

To serve, add all the tomatoes and diced onion to a bowl. Give everything a gentle toss. Crumble over the feta and finish with the dressing and basil leaves. Season again with salt and pepper and serve.

Overnight zhug bread

It's not pizza, it's not focaccia and it's not pide – but it is delicious. Do an overnight prove in the fridge to add a little funky flavour to the bread. You could let this slow-prove for up to three days in the fridge, but I am too impatient to wait that long for my carbs. It's important to preheat your oven before you get going on this one. The highest possible heat is key. **Serves 6–8**

Dough

1 × 7 g (¼ oz) sachet active dry yeast

very generous pinch of salt

2 tablespoons caster (superfine) sugar

2 tablespoons olive oil, plus extra for drizzling

375 ml (12½ fl oz/1½ cups) warm water

500 g (1 lb 2 oz) 00 flour (plus more on hand depending on how the dough is responding and for kneading)

To top

100 g (3½ oz) stracciatella

125 g (4½ oz/½ cup) Zhug (page 101)

coriander (cilantro) leaves

For the dough, add the dried yeast, a generous pinch of salt, the sugar, olive oil and warm water to a jug. Set aside for 15 minutes or until you see some bubbles on the surface of the mixture. If you don't see any activity it means your yeast is dead and it's important to start again here. If the weather is particularly cold, it may take a little longer for the bubbles to show.

Add the flour to the bowl of a stand mixer fitted with the dough hook. Add the warm water mixture and beat until a uniform dough forms. If after about 5 minutes it still feels too sticky, add a little more flour and beat until the dough appears smooth.

Transfer the dough to a large airtight container (it will increase in size) and place in the fridge overnight to prove.

Remove the dough from the fridge about 30 minutes before starting to cook and let stand at room temperature.

Preheat your oven to as high as it can go (285°C/545°F).

Stretch out the dough on a piece of baking paper to about the same size as a large heavy-based cast-iron pan (approximately 40 cm diameter) or heavy-based frying pan, creating a little bit of a border with thicker dough around the circumference. Add the stracciatella to the centre and spread it out, leaving a good 5 cm (2 in) border all the way around. Top with half the zhug and season generously with salt and freshly ground black pepper.

Heat the cast-iron pan or heavy-based frying pan over high heat until very hot. Drop the paper holding the dough into the frying pan and transfer the pan to the oven. Cook for about 7–10 minutes or until the dough is cooked through and risen around the edges and it looks puffed and deeply golden.

Drizzle with a little olive oil, dollop over the remaining zhug and scatter the coriander leaves on top. Season with salt and pepper and serve gloriously hot.

Barbecue sauce

 # Bloody useful red sauce

 # Caramel sauce

 # Lemon curd

Sauce of inspiration

Oh, how I could blab on about the virtues and importance of a decent sauce. I could go on and ON about how critical sauce is; a core building block that can make or break a dish. Chefs spend years, YEARS honing their craft as a saucier. A good sauce is a body-slam of flavour. It is a lighthouse; a shining beacon on the weeknight dinner culinary landscape that deserves your utmost care and attention. Because a good sauce is the kind you want to swim in. It's a feat of culinary engineering. Its aftershocks can take out a white shirt blindfolded at 10 paces and requires a baguette (at a minimum) to dredge and scrape any last evidence of its existence. Ultimately a good sauce leaves you feeling well cared for.

Barbecue sauce

There is nothing more beautiful than the scent of a good barbecue sauce. It's smouldering for the soul and quite primal. Made with love, time and stellar ingredients, a good barbecue sauce indicates a nerdy attention to detail, a heady mix of spices, and the balance of sweet, hot and smoky flavours. This is spoonable joy and can be applied to so many dishes. To think of barbecue and only think of meat dishes is reductive. While it's glorious slow-cooked into oblivion with beef, pork or chicken, it is a wonderful bedfellow for grains and tubers.

To make 1 litre
(34 fl oz/4 cups)

½ tbsp each: fennel seeds, cumin seeds, coriander seeds, celery seeds, mustard seeds and black peppercorns, all toasted in a dry pan until fragrant, then roughly ground

1 white onion, peeled and chopped

2 garlic cloves, peeled and chopped

2 tbsp olive oil

125 ml (4 fl oz/½ cup) apple juice

125 ml (4 fl oz/½ cup) apple cider vinegar

125 ml (4 fl oz/½ cup) honey mustard

125 ml (4 fl oz/½ cup) blackstrap molasses

125 ml (4 fl oz/½ cup) maple syrup

200 g (7 oz) tinned chopped tomatoes

150 g (5½ oz) excellent-quality apricot jam

70 g (2½ oz) tomato paste (concentrated purée)

1 chipotle in adobo

To make 2 litres
(68 fl oz/8 cups)

1 tbsp each: fennel seeds, cumin seeds, coriander seeds, celery seeds, mustard seeds and black peppercorns, all toasted in a dry pan until fragrant, then roughly ground

2 white onions, peeled and chopped

4 garlic cloves, peeled and chopped

60 ml (2 fl oz/¼ cup) olive oil

250 ml (8½ fl oz/1 cup) apple juice

250 ml (8½ fl oz/1 cup) apple cider vinegar

250 ml (8½ fl oz/1 cup) honey mustard

250 ml (8½ fl oz/1 cup) blackstrap molasses

250 ml (8½ fl oz/1 cup) maple syrup

400 g (14 oz) tinned chopped tomatoes

300 g (10½ oz) excellent-quality apricot jam

140 g (5 oz) tomato paste (concentrated purée)

2 chipotles in adobo

To make 3 litres
(101 fl oz/12 cups)

1½ tbsp each: fennel seeds, cumin seeds, coriander seeds, celery seeds, mustard seeds and black peppercorns, all toasted in a dry pan until fragrant, then roughly ground

3 white onions, peeled and chopped

6 garlic cloves, peeled and chopped

90 ml (3 fl oz) olive oil

375 ml (12½ fl oz/1½ cups) apple juice

375 ml (12½ fl oz/1½ cups) apple cider vinegar

375 ml (12½ fl oz/1½ cups) honey mustard

375 ml (12½ fl oz/1½ cups) blackstrap molasses

375 ml (12½ fl oz/1½ cups) maple syrup

600 g (1 lb 5 oz) tinned chopped tomatoes

450 g (1 lb) excellent-quality apricot jam

210 g (7½ oz) tomato paste (concentrated purée)

3 chipotles in adobo

Add the toasted spices, chopped onion and garlic to a food processor. Blitz until you have a paste-like mixture. You don't want to completely pulverise it, but you want a wet-style mixture.

Place a large saucepan over medium heat. Add the oil and, once shimmering, add the onion spice mix and cook, stirring regularly, for at least 10–15 minutes. You want the onion component to be thoroughly cooked through to ensure it doesn't taint your final sauce with a weird raw onion flavour. Add the remaining ingredients and turn the heat to low. Simmer, stirring regularly to prevent catching, for at least 30 minutes. You want it to have thickened and taste gloriously sweet, woody and smoky with a background herbaceous kind of profile. Season with salt and freshly ground black pepper.

Blitz the sauce with a stick blender in the pot, then pass it through a strainer for a gloriously smooth and silky sauce. Pour into sterilised bottles or screw-top jars. Once cool, store in the fridge for up to 6 months.

Barbecued roasted sweet potato and chickpea salad with feta, kale and crisp dolmades

Sauce of inspiration

This may seem an odd combination, but it is a good one. I love serving it while the sweet potato and dolmades are still warm. Turkish dolmas, known as *yaprak sarmasi*, usually contain a bit of tomato paste (concentrated purée) and pine nuts, whereas the Greek version, known as dolmades, contains more herbs, such as spring onions (scallions) and dill. Either will work here, but I find the Greek variety more readily available. **Serves 4 as part of a spread**

3 sweet potatoes, peeled and sliced lengthways into large wedges

125 ml (4 fl oz/½ cup) Barbecue sauce (page 114), plus 2 tablespoons extra to serve

3 tablespoons olive oil, plus extra to fry dolmades if needed

200 g (7 oz) tinned chickpeas, rinsed thoroughly and drained

8 dolmades or dolmas

75 g (2¾ oz/1 cup) thinly sliced cavolo nero (Tuscan kale)

75 g (2¾ oz/1 cup) very thinly sliced purple kale leaves

120 g (4½ oz/½ cup) crumbled Persian feta

coriander (cilantro) leaves, to scatter

Preheat the oven to 170°C (340°F).

Add the sweet potato to a large baking tray lined with baking paper. Add the barbecue sauce and olive oil and toss to coat. Season with salt and freshly ground black pepper, then roast in the oven for 30–45 minutes, turning the sweet potato halfway through cooking. It should be caramelised and golden at the edges and the flesh cooked through.

For the last 15 minutes of cooking time, add the chickpeas to the baking tray.

Place a frying pan over medium heat. Add a drizzle of olive oil – if you didn't purchase dolmades in oil – just enough to lightly coat the pan. Add the dolmades and cook for 1–3 minutes, or until warmed through and some of the vine leaves have taken on a crisp texture on the edges.

To serve, layer the sliced cavolo nero and purple kale leaves across the base of a serving plate. Top with the sweet potato slices and the roasted chickpeas. Scatter the feta over the top. Break a few of the dolmades over the salad, to spread some of the rice and vine mixture, then top the salad with remaining dolmades. Scatter with the coriander leaves and drizzle with the extra barbecue sauce. Season with salt and pepper and serve.

Barbecued roasted chicken with spiced whipped feta

We should embrace dips that become dinner. This can start as a snack, then be topped with sticky chicken and migrate you through a mealtime with ease. Crunchy, smoky, spicy and sweet. A real Trojan Horse of a dish.
Serves 4–6

1 organic free-range chicken, broken down into 4–8 pieces, depending on size of chicken

1 tablespoon brown sugar

1 tablespoon sweet smoked paprika

1 tablespoon salt

3 tablespoons olive oil

125 ml (4 fl oz/½ cup) Barbecue sauce (page 114), plus extra for basting

Whipped feta base

1 teaspoon ground coriander

1 teaspoon ground cumin

200 g (7 oz/¾ cup) crumbled Persian feta

100 g (3½ oz) crème fraîche

100 g (3½ oz) sour cream

Add the chicken pieces to a bowl with the sugar, paprika, salt, olive oil and barbecue sauce. Using your hands, toss to coat – you want the spices and oil to thoroughly coat the chicken. Set aside for 20 minutes to marinate.

For the whipped feta base, add all the ingredients to a food processor. Season with salt and freshly ground black pepper. Blend on high until smooth, about 2–3 minutes. Taste and adjust the seasoning if needed. Set aside. (You can make this in advance and store in the fridge – just make sure you bring it to room temperature before serving.)

Preheat the oven to 200°C (390°F).

Add the chicken to a roasting dish and bake for 15 minutes until it takes on a lovely colour. Reduce the heat to 180°C (360°F) and cook for a further 25 minutes or until the chicken is cooked through and the skin has taken on a glorious dark barbecue sauce–like colour. Halfway through cooking, baste the chicken in more of the barbecue sauce and turn the tray to ensure even roasting.

To serve, add the whipped feta to the base of a plate. Top with the chicken, season with salt and pepper and serve immediately. The chicken will warm the whipped feta and it will become gloriously swipeable and have rivers of barbecue sauce and chicken juice running through it. And it's a beautiful thing.

I often like to serve this with some warm bread so you don't miss any of the glorious juices, and a lovely crisp green salad like the Charred cos, buttermilk dressing, chicken salt breadcrumbs salad on page 36.

Za'atar barbecued lamb ribs

These ribs make a case for themselves just by sitting there, being crisp, hyper-sauced and brazen. Made only more glorious by the fact that the only way they should be eaten is with your hands, grabbing at bones, slipping on sauce, then burning the roof of your mouth on their piping-hot goodness. I serve these with the barbecued roasted sweet potatoes on page 116 or the sabiche salad on page 123. **Serves 6–8 as part of a spread**

1.2 kg (2 lb 10 oz) lamb ribs

125 ml (4 fl oz/½ cup) Barbecue sauce (page 114)

2 teaspoons za'atar, to sprinkle (optional)

Marinade

375 ml (12½ fl oz/1½ cups) Barbecue sauce

2 tablespoons za'atar

Preheat the oven to 200°C (390°F).

Combine the marinade ingredients in a large baking dish with 60 ml (2 fl oz/¼ cup) water. Add the ribs and give everything a decent slosh around in the dish – this will help prevent the ribs from sticking to the base of your roasting tray. Cover with baking paper and foil, seal as tightly as possible and bake for 1 hour. Remove the baking paper and foil and cook, uncovered, for another 30 minutes. You want the ribs to look caramelised – they should have taken on quite a bit of colour and a lot of oil will have seeped out.

Gently remove the ribs from the roasting tray and transfer to a large flat plate. Drizzle over some of the remaining barbecue sauce and the za'atar, if using, and turn to coat until the ribs are covered. Sprinkle with salt and serve with any remaining barbecue sauce.

Barbecue sauce

Double crisp barbecued potatoes

If you win at snacks with drinks, you win at life. It seems I have an insatiable need to pair potato with potato. Here the crisp skins and even crispier chips make wondrous, indulgent partners. Because the skins are the hero of the day, you can reserve the potato flesh for another dish. It makes for a brilliant breakfast - hash brown meets bubble 'n' squeak, or you could roast off the potato flesh and add it to the eggs all'amatriciana on page 21. **Serves 6 as a snack**

10–12 new potatoes

3 tablespoons olive oil

60–125 ml (¼–½ cup) Barbecue
   sauce (page 114)

To serve

60 g (2 oz/2 cups) excellent-quality
   potato chips (crisps)

125 ml (4 fl oz/½ cup) Barbecue
   sauce, for dipping

Halve the potatoes lengthways. Using a melon baller, scoop the potato flesh from the skins, trying not to puncture the skin. Reserve the potato flesh for another use.

Preheat the oven to 190°C (375°F).

Add the skins, olive oil and barbecue sauce to a large baking tray lined with baking paper. Using your hands, toss to coat, ensuring the potatoes are covered in oil and bits and blobs of barbecue sauce. Season generously with salt and freshly ground black pepper.

Roast for 10 minutes, then reduce the heat to 180°C (360°F) and roast for another 20–30 minutes or until the skins are crisp and golden. You want the skins to be crisp but need to ensure the sauce hasn't burned, giving the potatoes a bitter charred flavour. Turn the tray halfway through cooking.

When they look golden and crisp, add the skins to a serving platter and top with the potato chips. Serve with additional barbecue sauce on the side and watch them disappear.

Barbecued eggplant sabiche salad

Barbecue sauce-addled eggplant is a revelation. Join the cult with this salad, which is the perfect balance of crunch and chew, mouth-resisting firmness and yielding softness. It hits all the high points you could ever need in a salad. **Serves 4**

1 eggplant (aubergine), trimmed and sliced into 6 wedges lengthways

125 ml (4 fl oz/½ cup) Barbecue sauce (page 114)

1 tablespoon olive oil

500 ml (17 fl oz/2 cups) chicken or vegetable stock

185 g (6½ oz/¾ cup) burghul (bulgur wheat)

3–4 organic free-range eggs

1 cup each mint leaves, coriander (cilantro) leaves, flat-leaf (Italian) parsley leaves and young stems, all finely chopped

250 g (9 oz) cherry tomatoes, halved

1 small telegraph (long) cucumber, deseeded and sliced

za'atar, to scatter

Preheat the oven to 180°C (360°F).

Add the eggplant, barbecue sauce and olive oil to a bowl and, using your hands, toss to coat. Lay the pieces on a baking tray lined with baking paper and roast until the flesh is soft and has caramelised on the surface, between 25 and 40 minutes.

While the eggplant is cooking, bring the stock to the boil. Put the burghul in a bowl, pour over the hot stock and let sit for 15 minutes. Strain any residual liquid and immediately season the burghul with salt and freshly ground black pepper.

Add the eggs to a saucepan of cold water. Bring to the boil and cook for 10 minutes. Run the eggs under running water and gently peel the shells. Halve the eggs. Season with salt immediately.

Tip the burghul into a bowl and allow to cool before adding all the chopped herbs. Tip onto a serving platter. Top with the barbecued eggplant wedges, cherry tomatoes and sliced cucumber. Add the cooked eggs and scatter with the za'atar.

Barbecue sauce

Bulk it out

- Add hummus to the base of the plate before adding everything on top
- Add some toasted pita bread either directly to the salad or as a side for scooping

Bloody useful red sauce

This is pure comfort food. It's simple, honest, and doesn't leave a single person in the room behind. It's the first recipe I want my kids to learn by rote and by taste. It's exactly what you make when you need to nourish yourself and your tribe. It's the recipe you turn to when you need a base; and proof that true luxury doesn't need to be expensive. I've presumed this to be one of the most broadly used sauces and have provided for a rather large quantity. Find a bloody big pot. You are going to need it.

To make 3.5 litres
(118 fl oz)

60 ml (2 fl oz/¼ cup) olive oil

4 brown onions, chopped

8 garlic cloves, minced

½ bunch oregano, leaves picked and chopped

60 g (2 oz) smoked pancetta, in one piece

1 parmesan rind

½ tablespoon salt

½ tablespoon black peppercorns

300 g (10½ oz) tomato paste (concentrated purée)

250 ml (8½ fl oz/1 cup) red wine

1.2 kg (2 lb 10 oz) tinned chopped tomatoes

1.2 kg (2 lb 10 oz) beefsteak tomatoes, cored, peeled and chopped

½ tbsp sweet smoked paprika

40 g (1½ oz) brown sugar

500 ml (17 fl oz/2 cups) chicken stock

To make 7 litres
(236 fl oz)

120 ml (4 fl oz) olive oil

8 brown onions, chopped (about 1 kg/2 lb 3 oz)

16 garlic cloves, minced

1 bunch oregano, leaves picked and chopped

150 g (5½ oz) smoked pancetta, in one piece

1–2 parmesan rinds

1 tbsp salt

1 tbsp black peppercorns, lightly ground

600 g (1 lb 5 oz) tomato paste (concentrated purée)

2 cups (17 fl oz/500 ml) red wine

2.4 kg (5½ lb) tinned chopped tomatoes

2.4 kg (5½ lb) beefsteak tomatoes, cored, peeled, chopped

1 tbsp sweet smoked paprika

100 g (3½ oz) brown sugar

1 litre (34 fl oz/4 cups) chicken stock

To make 14 litres
(472 fl oz)

240 ml (8 fl oz) olive oil

16 brown onions, chopped (about 2 kg/4 lb 6 oz)

32 garlic cloves, minced

2 bunches oregano, leaves picked and chopped

300 g (10½ oz) smoked pancetta, in one piece

2-3 parmesan rinds

2 tbsp salt

2 tbsp black peppercorns, lightly ground

1.2 kg (2 lb 10 oz) tomato paste

4 cups (34 fl oz/1 litre) red wine

4.8 kg (10 lb) tinned chopped tomatoes

4.8 kg (10 lb) beefsteak tomatoes, cored, peeled, chopped

2 tbsp sweet smoked paprika

200 g (7 oz) brown sugar

2 litres (68 fl oz/ 8 cups) chicken stock

Heat the olive oil in a large heavy-based saucepan over medium-high heat.
Add the onion and garlic and cook, stirring regularly, for 10 minutes.

Add the oregano, pancetta, parmesan rind, salt and peppercorns and continue to cook
over medium heat for a further 8–10 minutes, until the onion is completely soft and
lightly caramelised.

Stir in the tomato paste and cook for a further 3–4 minutes, then add the remaining
ingredients. Reduce the heat to low and simmer gently for 3–4 hours, until the sauce has
reduced and is thick and rich.

Remove the pancetta and whatever is left of the parmesan rind and discard.
Lightly blend the sauce with a stick blender.

Continue to reduce the sauce over low heat for a further 30–50 minutes until thick
and dark red. Remove from the heat, check the seasoning and cool ready for use.
This will keep for up to 3 months refrigerated in tightly sealed jars.

It's not just another eggplant parmy

Okay, it is. But this eggplant parmy (aubergine parmigiana/eggplant parm) is like a hug from Nonna. Since you've already done the hard work making the sauce, this is a light frying, assembling, and shoving in the oven sort of dinner. Just don't rush the oven part – you want it brown and properly bubbling on top. It also makes the kind of leftovers you can look forward to. Even for breakfast. Add a fried egg. A heft of chilli flakes. Go large. **Serves 6**

750 ml (25½ fl oz/3 cups) Bloody useful red sauce (page 124)

700 ml (24 fl oz) tomato passata

3 eggplants/aubergines, (approx. 1.2 kg/2 lb 10 oz)

3 large organic free-range eggs

320 g (11½ oz/4 cups) fresh sourdough breadcrumbs

hefty pinch each of chilli flakes, dried oregano, dried basil and brown sugar

olive oil, for frying

1 ball buffalo mozzarella (approx. 150 g/5½ oz), grated

1 bunch basil, leaves picked

100 g (3½ oz/1 cup) shaved parmesan

Tip

• You may need to wipe the frying pan clean after every other round to prevent cooking burnt breadcrumbs and ruining the taste of your parmy.

Preheat the oven to 180°C (360°F).

Combine the bloody useful sauce and tomato passata in a large saucepan and place over low heat. Stir to combine and let it sit on the stove to warm through while you prep the eggplant.

Slice the eggplants into 1 cm (½ in) thick slices. Whisk the eggs in a bowl. In a separate bowl combine the breadcrumbs, dried spices, herbs and sugar. Season generously with salt and freshly ground black pepper.

Coat each eggplant slice with the egg mixture, then the breadcrumbs and set aside on a clean board or plate.

Once all the eggplant has been crumbed, add enough olive oil to generously coat a large frying pan and place over medium heat. Allow to heat until shimmering, then fry the eggplant in batches – you want to cook it for about 2 minutes on each side, or until the crumbed edge is golden.

To assemble the parmy, ladle some sauce into the base of a large ovenproof dish and spread to cover. Add a layer of eggplant and scatter over some cheese and basil leaves. Keep repeating with the eggplant and sauce, finishing with a generous layer of sauce and cheese.

Cover with foil and bake in the oven for about 1 hour. Remove the foil and cook for an additional 30 minutes or until the cheese has turned crisp in spots and darkened and you have lovely potholes of bubbling sauce.

You must let this rest for a good 10 minutes on the bench before serving. If not, it will go everywhere. And all those layers you worked on will be ruined. Sit tight, the wait is worth it.

Serve with a green salad and some bread for plate mopping.

She sure is saucy chicken puttanesca

Puttanesca. One of my favourite words. And this is probably one of my favourite dishes. **Serves 6**

3 tablespoons olive oil

900 g (2 lb) chicken thighs, skin on, bone removed

1 onion, peeled and sliced

2 garlic cloves, chopped

2–3 anchovies, chopped

generous pinch of chilli flakes

375 ml (12½ fl oz/1½ cups) rosé

375 ml (12½ fl oz/1½ cups) Bloody useful red sauce (page 124)

180 g (1 cup) green olives, pitted

3 tablespoons capers

½ cup chopped flat-leaf (Italian) parsley, to serve

grated parmesan, to serve (optional)

Place a large non-stick frying pan over medium heat. Add 2 tablespoons of the olive oil and, once hot, place the chicken, skin side down, in the frying pan. You might like to weight the chicken down with a plate or smaller saucepan – it helps to really render the fat, crisp the chicken skin and give it an even golden tan. Cook for 5–7 minutes or until the skin is lovely and crisp. Gently flip the chicken and add the onion and cook for 1–2 minutes in the rendered chicken fat until soft and translucent, then add the garlic and anchovies. Add the chilli and turn the heat to low.

Pour the rosé and the bloody useful red sauce around the chicken. Add the olives, stir them through and simmer for 20–25 minutes. You want the sauce to have thickened and reduced slightly and the chicken to be cooked through.

While the chicken is cooking, place a small frying pan over medium heat. Add the remaining olive oil and, once hot, fry the capers until crisp and they have begun to open out like flowers. Use a slotted spoon to remove them from the pan and scatter them over the chicken.

Season the chicken, then add the chopped parsley. Serve with the parmesan (if using).

Prawn saganaki with feta, fennel and ouzo

I'm a sucker for a barbecued prawn, so I like to add them to the sauce straight from the grill at the last moment. If you prefer a more traditional method, add the prawns with the ouzo and feta and cook until the meat is just white and no longer translucent, 5–7 minutes. No matter how many times I make this dish, I'm astounded by how great it tastes with such little effort. It would be criminal to serve without hunks of bread for mopping and wine for glugging. **Serves 4–6**

4 tablespoons olive oil

1 fennel bulb, finely chopped, fronds (and flowers if it has some) reserved

3 garlic cloves, chopped

3 fresh red chillies, deseeded and chopped

1 teaspoon anise seeds, crushed

750 ml (25½ fl oz/3 cups) Bloody useful red sauce (page 124)

125–250 ml (4–8½ fl oz/½–1 cup) white wine, for thinning

3–4 tablespoons ouzo

200 g (7 oz) Persian feta

16 large prawns (shrimp), peeled and deveined

chopped flat-leaf (Italian) parsley, to serve

Preheat the oven to 180°C (360°F).

Warm a frying pan over medium heat. When hot, add the olive oil followed by the fennel, garlic, chillies and anise seeds. Season generously with salt and freshly ground black pepper, lower the heat as low as it can go and cover the pan. Cook for about 15–20 minutes, or until sweet, golden and fragrant. Add the bloody useful red sauce and simmer to incorporate the flavours for 5 minutes or so. If you are concerned your sauce is overly thick (as in it has reduced significantly on the stovetop) don't panic, just thin out with 125–250 ml (½–1 cup) white wine as needed.

If you are a forward planner you can stop here. Prep the sauce and have it ready to throw the prawns in and finish the dish later in the week.

Scoop the sauce into an ovenproof dish. Stir through the ouzo and add the chunks of feta. Pop in the oven and cook until warmed through and the feta has melted into indecent-looking glorious globs of cream, about 10–15 minutes.

While the sauce is cooking, brush a barbecue hotplate with oil and bring to medium-high heat. Barbecue the prawns, cooking for 1–2 minutes each side until the meat is white and no longer translucent.

Remove the sauce from the oven and top with the prawns, pushing the prawns down into the glorious sauce until partially submerged and sprinkle with the chopped parsley, and the reserved fennel fronds and flowers, if using. Serve immediately.

Slow-roasted lamb shoulder with fried caper gremolata

Cook 'em low, cook 'em slow. The reward for such little effort really is mind boggling. I like to roast this and then transfer the lamb to its bloody useful sauce bath for the last hour of braising, uncovered, so the two can become perfectly acquainted. **Serves 8**

1 × 2 kg (4 lb 6 oz) lamb shoulder, bone in

2 tablespoons olive oil

3 oregano sprigs, leaves picked

3 rosemary sprigs, leaves picked

6 garlic cloves, roughly chopped

250 ml (8½ fl oz/1 cup) white wine

500 ml (17 fl oz/2 cups) chicken stock

750 ml (25½ fl oz/3 cups) Bloody useful red sauce (page 124)

Fried caper gremolata

2 tablespoons olive oil

3 tablespoons capers

2 garlic cloves, finely chopped

3 tablespoons flat-leaf (Italian) parsley, finely chopped

2 tablespoons finely chopped basil

zest of 2 unwaxed lemons

Preheat the oven to 150°C (300°F).

Put the lamb in a large casserole dish.

Add the oil into a small food processor and add the oregano, rosemary and garlic. Whizz to a rough paste. Season the paste well with salt and freshly ground black pepper, then rub the mixture all over the lamb.

Pour the wine and stock around the base of the lamb, trying not to wash the paste from the top. Cover very tightly with foil and roast for 5 hours, topping with stock or water if the liquid is evaporating too rapidly.

Add the bloody useful red sauce to another casserole dish.

When the lamb has been roasting for 4 hours, gently remove from the oven then, using a spatula and tongs, carefully transfer the lamb to the casserole dish with the sauce. Place in the oven and roast, uncovered, for the last hour.

While the lamb is cooking, prepare the caper gremolata. Add the olive oil to a small frying pan over medium heat. Once the oil is shimmering, add the capers and fry, tossing often to prevent catching, until the capers are crisp and have spread out like flowers. Add the garlic and cook until just fragrant. Transfer to a bowl. Once cooled slightly, add the remaining ingredients and toss to combine. Season.

To serve, transfer the entire roasting dish to the table. Top the lamb with the fried caper gremolata, then let people help themselves. The meat will pull away easily from the bone.

Bloody useful red sauce

Broken sleep soup with crispy smoked olive arancini

This is the kind of meal that feeds the soul as well as the belly. I've also engineered it to be a gift that keeps on giving. The arancini recipe makes more than you need for this dish, so you can stash it in the freezer for a last-minute meal at ANY time. I suggest strongly that you do. **Serves 4**

375 ml (12½ fl oz/1½ cups) Bloody useful red sauce (page 124)

250–500 ml (8½–17 fl oz/1–2 cups) passata (depending on how thick your Bloody useful red sauce is)

chicken stock, if needed to thin the sauce

4 tablespoons mascarpone

basil leaves and oregano leaves, to scatter

Arancini

2 tablespoons olive oil

1 onion, diced

2 garlic cloves, crushed

115 g (4 oz) smoked kalamata olives, chopped

220 g (8 oz) arborio or carnaroli rice

250 ml (8½ fl oz/1 cup) white wine

500 g (1 lb 2 oz/2 cups) chicken stock

100 g (3½ oz) gruyère, grated

100 g (3½ oz) cheddar, grated

75 g (2¾ oz) flour

2 large organic free-range eggs, lightly whisked

150 g (5½ oz) dry breadcrumbs

To make the arancini, heat the olive oil in a pressure cooker or in a saucepan over medium heat. Add the onion and cook until pale and translucent. Add the garlic and chopped olives and cook until fragrant. Add the rice and cook until toasted, about 1–2 minutes. Add the wine and stock. If using your pressure cooker, add all the wine and stock at once and set to the risotto function and cook for 12–14 minutes.

Alternatively, if using the stovetop method, add the stock gradually, and cook for 15–20 minutes, stirring regularly and adding the wine and stock until the rice is cooked through. Stir the cheeses through until melted. Remove the rice and pop in the fridge, uncovered, for an hour or so, or until the rice has cooled, feels lightly sticky and is easy to handle.

Preheat the oven to 180°C (360°F).

Roll the risotto into balls, approximately the size of golf balls. Roll the balls in flour, then beaten egg, followed by the breadcrumbs to coat, shaking off any excess. Place on a baking tray lined with baking paper and bake for 20 minutes, turning gently halfway through to get a nice even brown crust.

To make the soup, add the bloody useful red sauce and passata to a medium saucepan over medium heat. Cook, stirring often to prevent catching, until warmed through. If it seems too thick, you can thin it out with a dash of stock. Season with salt and freshly ground black pepper. Scoop into bowls, add a dollop of mascarpone and top with 2–3 arancini per serve. You can halve these and scatter over the top. Add a few basil and oregano leaves and serve.

Drunk pasta

When I lived in New York for a red-hot minute, I threw financial caution to the wind and ate at Mario Batali's restaurant Babbo's – there was a bit of a cult special - this vermouth pasta served with a negroni neat, and my lordy it was food-memory-altering good. And I feel we should all embrace its deliciousness and this wee version has it in spades with: 1. Sweet jammy roasted shallots. 2. A hit of gin and vermouth/campari. 3. Carbs. 4. The first three together. All at the same time. It's the recipe to make when you have nothing and everything to prove. It is so understated in its glorious mess yet so articulate in flavour and je ne sais quoi. **Serves 4**

500 g (1 lb 2 oz) French shallots, halved lengthways

90 ml (3 fl oz) olive oil

5 garlic cloves, peeled

750 ml (25½ fl oz/3 cups) Bloody useful red sauce (page 124)

90 ml (3 fl oz) Campari or vermouth

85 ml (2¾ fl oz) gin

500 g (1 lb 2 oz) large dried rigatoni

250 g (9 oz) buffalo mozzarella coarsely torn

Preheat the oven to 170°C (340°F).

Add the shallots, 60 ml (¼ cup) of the olive oil and the garlic to a baking tray lined with baking paper. Toss to coat. Cover the tray with foil and roast for 20 minutes. Remove the foil and roast for a further 20 minutes or until the shallots are very soft and have taken on a glorious dark roasted colour.

Place a large saucepan over medium heat. Add the remaining olive oil and, once shimmering, add the roasted shallots and garlic and the bloody useful red sauce. Reduce the heat to low, add the vermouth and gin and let the flavours get acquainted. You want to give it at least 15 minutes – 20 would be nicer – or until the sauce appears to have reduced a little and thickened. Take two forks and shred the very soft shallots into the sauce. This doesn't need to be perfect, just pulling them apart enough to ensure their goodness is spread through the sauce is all that is required.

Add the pasta to a large pot of boiling water and cook for 5 minutes – you don't want to cook the pasta all the way through. Strain and run under cold water briefly. Reserve some of the pasta water.

Grease a round 25 cm baking dish and smear the base with about ½ cup of the sauce. Stand the rigatoni in it until full then gently pour in some of the sauce, using a spoon to smear and fill the holes. Gently push pieces of mozzarella into the pasta here and there – little surprises of cheese ooze waiting to be found. You want enough sauce in and around the rigatoni so it can finish cooking in the oven – if you seem short on sauce, just top with a little water. Season generously and pop in the oven for 30 minutes or until cooked and the top is bubbling.

Scatter over parmesan and serve.

Spag in a bag

Prepare your parcels. Organise thy life. The true glory of this dish (also known as spaghetti al cartoccio) is the pre-prep. You cook the pasta; slop in some Bloody useful red sauce; transfer to baking paper bags; top with seafood. Then, when you are ready to go, bang it in the oven. If I was hiring a luxurious beachside abode and had throngs of friends, I'd invite them over for too many glasses of le vin and cook this dish. **Serves 4–6**

500 g (1 lb 2 oz) dried spaghetti

500 ml (17 fl oz/2 cups) Bloody
   useful red sauce (page 124)

600 g (1 lb 5 oz) fresh mixed
   seafood (I used calamari/squid,
   prawns/shrimp, blue-eye cod)

a few knobs of unsalted butter
   (approx. 1 oz/25–30 g), cubed

2–3 sprigs lemon thyme,
   leaves picked

olive oil

generous pinch of chilli flakes,
   or to taste

zest of 1 unwaxed lemon

Preheat the oven to 180°C (360°F).

Bring a large pot of water to the boil and season heavily with salt. Add the spaghetti and cook until just shy of al dente. Strain briefly and return to the pot – any residual pasta cooking water is a win here. Add the bloody useful red sauce, turning to coat.

Add a sheet of baking paper to a rimmed baking tray. Plop the pasta in the centre of the sheet of baking paper (or smaller amounts if making individual serves).

Top with your chosen seafood, the cubes of butter and the lemon thyme. Season very generously with salt and freshly ground black pepper. Bring the sides of your paper to the centre and tie firmly with a piece of kitchen string.

Cook in the oven for 7–12 minutes. Remove and open the paper carefully as quite a lot of steam will escape. Check the seafood is cooked through. Drizzle with some olive oil and sprinkle with the chilli flakes and lemon zest and serve in the bag at the table.

Don't overthink it

While French chefs love their *en papillote* perfection, I've seen too many people make intricate parcels by folding paper and reinforcing with foil, only to have the ingredients leach out everywhere and ruin the dish. Just throw the spaghetti in the middle of the paper, draw up the sides and tie with string like it's a Christmas pudding. Gather all your skills of wrapping an awkwardly shaped present and apply here. No intricate folding and hoping for the best required.

Caramel

I remember watching my grandmother make caramel. Her hands – gosh those hands – toughened by years working on the land but so gentle when it came to anything she touched on the hob. In later years, I would watch her hand shake ever so slightly as she placed the clumped sugar into the pan, her paper-thin skin stretched taut, chuckling as the caramel foamed and hissed. To this day I am felled by the power of this simple indulgence, the comfort embedded in this simple sauce's golden hues. What seems a simple recipe needs love, care and attention to reach its full potential. Success is in the detail, so do not look away for a moment.

To make 500 ml
(17 fl oz/2 cups)

340 g (12 oz) caster (superfine) sugar

125 g (4½ oz) excellent-quality unsalted butter, at room temperature, cut into small cubes

175 ml (6 fl oz) pouring (single/light) cream

2 tsp sea salt flakes

To make 1 litre
(34 fl oz/4 cups)

675 g (1½ lb) caster (superfine) sugar

250 g (9 oz) excellent-quality unsalted butter, at room temperature, cut into small cubes

355 ml (11½ fl oz) pouring (single/light) cream

1 tbsp sea salt flakes

To make 1.5 litres
(51 fl oz/6 cups)

1 kg (2 lb 3 oz) caster (superfine) sugar

375 g (13 oz) excellent-quality unsalted butter, at room temperature, cut into small cubes

530 ml (18 fl oz) pouring (single/light) cream

1 tbsp sea salt flakes

In a heavy-based saucepan over medium–low heat, heat the sugar until it has completely melted – swirl the pan gently every 20 seconds. The sugar will clump in spots before melting slowly. Watch this part closely – it's important not to let it burn.

Once melted, remove from the heat and whisk in the butter – your mixture will look as though it is possessed, violently bubbling. Continue whisking until the bubbles begin to subside.

Slowly pour in the cream and half the salt. Whisk until everything is combined.
Taste a spoonful of the caramel – if it is mouth-cloyingly sweet, add the rest of the salt.

Allow to cool completely before using.

If you'd like to add vanilla, I suggest adding it separately, so you have some caramel in reserve for savoury dishes. To add vanilla, simply add 1 tablespoon of vanilla bean extract for every 500 ml (17 fl oz/2 cups) of caramel.

Caramel can be stored in jars with a screw-top lid. It will last for 6 weeks in the fridge and up to 4 months in the freezer.

Tips for the best home-made caramel

- Use high-quality butter. You're only as good as your ingredients and with caramel your butter quality can really make or break your sauce. This is one time when it's a good idea to splurge on that packet that's a few dollars more.

- Never leave your caramel sauce unattended. To make caramel sauce you essentially toast white sugar until it's melted, before adding in butter, cream and salt. Your sugar can go from toasty to burnt in the blink of an eye - watch, watch, watch.

- Don't forget the salt! Caramel is simply too sweet without it. A healthy amount of salt really deepens the flavour profile.

Roasted carrot and parsnip salad with feta, caramel and crunchy bits

This is honey-roasted carrots for a new age with parsnip for earthy depth. The caramel ensures a gloriously sweet – you guessed it – caramelisation of the root vegetables, with the salty hit of feta and pop of amaranth making this a low-key, yet balanced, plate of heaven. **Serves 4–6**

1 bunch heirloom carrots, washed, tops trimmed

3 parsnips, trimmed and quartered lengthways (peeling optional)

2 tablespoons olive oil

2 tablespoons Caramel (page 138)

Dressing

1½ tablespoons Caramel

1 tablespoon sherry vinegar

1½ tablespoons olive oil

To finish

120 g (4½ oz) crumbled Persian feta

130 g (4½ oz) smoked almonds, chopped

3 tablespoons puffed amaranth (see Note) (if unavailable, use puffed quinoa)

Preheat the oven to 180°C (360°F).

Add the carrots and parsnips to a rimmed baking tray and drizzle with the oil and caramel. Using your hands, toss the vegetables to coat them evenly in the mixture. Add 3–4 tablespoons of water and cover the tray tightly in foil. Roast until the vegetables have cooked through, around 25–30 minutes. Remove the foil and roast for an additional 20–30 minutes so they become lovely and caramelised. Keep an eye on them at this point, and remove from the oven if they are taking on too much colour.

For the dressing, add the ingredients to a small saucepan and place over low heat to warm through. Stir to combine, ensuring the ingredients are fully incorporated.

Remove the carrots and parsnips from the oven. Gently transfer to a serving plate and sprinkle over the feta and chopped almonds. Drizzle with the dressing and season generously with salt and freshly ground black pepper. Sprinkle with the puffed amaranth and serve immediately.

Caramel

Notes

- Puffed amaranth is available from most health food stores.
- Make the granola on page 63 and throw in any leftover puffed amaranth for epic breakfast goodness.

Guinness chocolate 'n' caramel cake of the gods

Intense, strong and refined. This, in my mind, is the perfect cake. It has depth, without any cloying sweetness, and only improves after a few days sitting on the outskirts of your kitchen bench. There is currently a trend for heavy, brownie-like cakes that verge on sludge, but not this one. While it's definitely still a chocolate cake, it has a beautiful lightness to it. The Guinness is the perfect foil to the sweetness of the caramel and rather lofty heights of icing that crown it. **Makes 12–16 slices**

Cake

250 ml (8½ fl oz/1 cup) Guinness

250 g (9 oz) unsalted butter

80 g (2¾ oz/⅓ cup) Dutch (unsweetened) cocoa powder

300 g (10½ oz) caster (superfine) sugar

100 ml (3½ fl oz) Caramel (page 138), plus extra to serve

2 large organic free-range eggs

½ tablespoon vanilla bean paste

140 ml (4½ fl oz) buttermilk

280 g (10 oz) plain (all-purpose) flour

2 teaspoons bicarbonate of soda (baking soda)

pinch of salt

½ teaspoon baking powder

Buttercream

180 g (6½ oz) organic free-range egg whites (about 6 eggs)

230 g (8 oz/1 cup) caster (superfine) sugar

350 g (12½ oz) unsalted butter, soft at room temperature,

4 tablespoons Dutch (unsweetened) cocoa powder

pinch of salt

125 ml (4 fl oz/½ cup) Caramel, to drizzle

Preheat the oven to 170°C (340°F). Line the base of a 23 cm diameter, minimum 10cm deep, round springform cake tin.

Add the Guinness and butter to a saucepan and place over low heat until the butter has melted. Remove from the heat and stir through the cocoa powder and sugar.

Mix together the caramel, eggs, vanilla and buttermilk in a bowl, then add the Guinness mixture, stirring to combine.

Sift the remaining cake ingredients into the bowl of a stand mixer fitted with the paddle attachment. Pour the Guinness mixture into the bowl of the stand mixer set on low speed. Scrape down the side of the bowl and mix thoroughly until all the ingredients are incorporated. Stir through the caramel.

Pour the batter into the prepared cake tin and bake for 45 minutes or until a skewer inserted into the middle of the cake comes out clean. Set aside to cool, then remove from the tin and transfer to a wire rack, to cool completely.

For the buttercream, put the egg whites and sugar in the bowl of a stand mixer set over a saucepan filled with water. Over medium heat, whisk constantly, until the mixture reaches 71°C (160°F). The sugar will be dissolved and the mixture hot to the touch. Immediately remove the bowl from the heat, and fix the bowl onto the stand mixer fitted with the whisk attachment.

Whisk on high speed until a thick and glossy meringue has formed, 5–7 minutes. Beat in the butter, a tablespoon at a time. Lower the speed and add the cocoa powder and salt. Continue to beat until silky-smooth and aerated. Generously scoop the buttercream onto the cake. You can either frost the entire cake or add voluptuous pillows of icing to the top. Gently drizzle with caramel and slice to serve.

No-churn salted caramel ice cream

This is ridiculous. So easy. So good. I'm not sure you'd bother making ice cream from scratch with all the egg-heating, custard-creating shenanigans ever again. The olive oil adds a beautiful mouthfeel to this ice cream, and don't panic, you won't notice the flavour – no one wants ice cream that tastes like a salad dressing. **Serves 8**

600 ml (20½ fl oz) thickened (whipping) cream

375 ml (12½ fl oz/1½ cups) sweetened condensed milk

3 tablespoons olive oil

smoked salt, to taste

250 ml (8½ fl oz/1 cup) Caramel (page 138)

In a large bowl using hand-held electric mixers, or in a stand mixer fitted with the whisk attachment, whisk the cream to stiff peaks. Add the sweetened condensed milk, olive oil and smoked salt. Whisk briefly – you want the ingredients to only just be incorporated.

Pour the mixture into a loaf (bar) tin or freezer-proof container. Once poured, gently fold the caramel into the whipped cream mixture. Add any mix ins, if using. Don't overmix – this looks best when you get rough swirls of caramel. Sprinkle with more smoked salt. Pop in the freezer for 3–4 hours or until set. If you don't want to use it immediately, it helps to cover the ice cream with baking paper to prevent freezer burn, then give it a double wrap with foil to help prevent any icicles from forming.

Mix ins

Roasted strawberry and pink peppercorn: Sprinkle some strawberries with balsamic vinegar and roast until soft and a touch caramelised. Add some lightly crushed pink peppercorns.

Nougat, raspberry and lavender: Chopped nougat, some freeze-dried raspberries and lavender.

Coffee choc flake: A few roughly crushed coffee beans and some flaked chocolate – milk or dark, whichever floats your boat.

Chocolate brownie: Heavy on the sea salt, nothing better than soft fudgy chunks of brownie and flakes of salt to offset the sweet.

Togarashi caramel beef skewers

Food on sticks. The end. Start this the day before, for maximum juicy marinating action. **Serves 6**

½ onion, coarsely chopped

2 garlic cloves, coarsely chopped

2 tablespoons Caramel (page 138)

2 teaspoons togarashi seasoning

1 kg (2 lb 3 oz) beef (sirloin works well), cut into even-sized cubes

To serve

2 limes, halved

60 ml (2 fl oz/¼ cup) Caramel

togarashi seasoning

Process the onion and garlic in a small food processor until finely chopped, then add the oil and process to a paste. Add the caramel and togarashi, season to taste with salt and process to combine.

Add to a large bowl with the beef, stirring to coat the meat well. Refrigerate to marinate overnight – or at least for a good few hours if time and the desire for preplanning preclude a sleepover in the fridge.

Preheat a barbecue or chargrill pan to high heat. Thread the beef pieces onto metal skewers (leave a little space in between so the beef can brown) and cook, turning regularly to prevent the caramel from burning, until browned and cooked to your liking, 3–4 minutes for medium. Add the limes, flesh side down, to the side and cook until they have taken on a little colour.

Season the beef with salt and a little extra togarashi.

Serve the beef with the charred limes and extra caramel and togarashi on the side. These are best when piping hot – they also go down a treat with some steamed rice, and veggies given a similar treatment to the beef.

Date slab with bourbon caramel

The elixir here is half a kilo of dates in one little cake and the bourbon addition to the Caramel. It's also two bowls, a 'quick-stir-and-done' sort of baking, no aerating of batters requiring mixers and attachments. It's quick 'n' dirty, and factors in the importance of immediacy. **Serves 12**

500 g (1 lb 2 oz) dried (or fresh) pitted dates

2 teaspoons bicarbonate of soda (baking soda)

550 ml (18½ fl oz) boiling water

2 teaspoons vanilla bean paste

165 g (6 oz) caster (superfine) sugar

165 g (6 oz/¾ cup, firmly packed) brown sugar

2 organic free-range eggs

270 g (9½ oz) plain (all-purpose) flour

2 teaspoons baking powder

310 ml (10½ fl oz/1¼ cups) Caramel (page 138)

1 tablespoon smoky bourbon

ice cream, to serve (optional)

Preheat the oven to 170°C (340°F). Butter a 25 x 35 cm (10 x 14 in) glass or metal baking dish.

Add the dates to a bowl with the bicarbonate of soda. Pour the boiling water over and set aside until the dates look pulpy and soft, about 10 minutes. Add the dates and soaking liquid to a food processor and blitz briefly – this is just to get rid of any random residual chunky bits.

Combine the vanilla, sugars and eggs in a large bowl and whisk until the mixture is smooth and you get ribbons when you lift up a spoon of mixture. Add the date mixture and mix to fully incorporate. Add the flour, baking powder and a pinch of salt and gently fold this mixture through the date mixture until just incorporated.

Pour the batter into the dish and bake for about 35–45 minutes, or until a skewer inserted in the centre comes out clean. Allow to cool in the dish for at least 40 minutes before serving.

Using a skewer, poke multiple holes across the surface of the cake. Pour over about 185–250 ml (¾–1 cup) caramel, spreading it across the cake and into the holes you created with the skewer. Cover with plastic wrap and set aside for the cake to absorb the glorious caramel.

When ready to serve, add the remaining caramel and bourbon to a saucepan and place over low heat. Warm through and whisk to ensure the bourbon is fully incorporated.

Slice the slab into generous squares. Drizzle over some of the bourbon caramel and serve or also add a generous dollop of ice cream for that extra hedonistic pleasure.

Caramel

Lemon curd

Lemon curd is something you should never buy in a jar. I'll bend this rule if you buy it from a school fete or hospital fundraiser where a home cook has whisked their forearm away in the name of charity. Otherwise, nothing compares to a bag of lemons, some butter, sugar, plenty of eggs and a little bit of your time. Lemon curd can form a multitude of desserts; it can be slathered across a chicken. It can be served at breakfast as well as the celebratory end to a great meal. A good Lemon curd is everything.

To make 500 ml	To make 1 litre	To make 1.5 litres
(17 fl oz/2 cups)	(34 fl oz/4 cups)	(51 fl oz/6 cups)
170 g (6 oz/⅔ cup) caster sugar	340 g (12 oz/1⅓ cup) caster sugar	510 g (1 lb 2 oz) caster (superfine) sugar
80 g (2¾ oz) chilled unsalted butter	160 g (5½ oz) chilled unsalted butter	240 g (9 oz) chilled unsalted butter, cut into cubes
zest and juice of 2 unwaxed lemons	zest and juice of 4 unwaxed lemons	zest and juice of 6 unwaxed lemons
½ tbsp vanilla bean paste	1 tbsp vanilla bean paste	2 tbsp vanilla bean paste
2 organic free-range eggs, plus 2 egg yolks	4 organic free-range eggs, plus 4 egg yolks	6 organic free-range eggs, plus 6 egg yolks

Whisk the sugar, butter, lemon zest and juice, and vanilla in a saucepan over medium–low heat. Once incorporated, turn the heat to low and whisk in the whole eggs and yolks. Whisk continually until thickened and the curd coats the back of a spoon. Strain through a sieve and store in a jar until ready to use. Any leftovers will last up to 3 weeks in the fridge.

Lemon curd, coconut ice cream, finger lime and makrut basil sugar

Once the curd is made, this throw-together dessert defines minimum effort, maximum taste. The grassy notes of basil and makrut lime relieve the richness of this dessert and the finger lime enlivens the palate. It is all brightness, ease, and summertime fun, just like you (and occasionally me). The recipe below can be scaled up. **Serves 1**

80–125 g (2¾ oz–4½ oz/⅓–½ cup)
Lemon curd (page 151) per person

1 scoop excellent-quality coconut
ice cream per serve

red finger lime pearls, to serve
(I aim for the pearls of ½ finger
lime per serve) (if unavailable,
replace with the zest of
1 unwaxed lime)

Makrut basil sugar

115 g (4 oz/½ cup) caster (superfine)
sugar

¼ cup firmly packed basil leaves

3 makrut lime leaves, deveined and
roughly chopped

To make the makrut basil sugar, put the ingredients in a small food processor or grinder. Process until even and fine, stopping before the mixture turns into damp clumps – it shouldn't take more than 20 seconds. You want to see variations in the mixture – you want to see sugar, green and a mixed combination of the two. It's perfectly imperfect this way.

Spoon the lemon curd into a serving bowl. Top with a scoop of coconut ice cream and sprinkle over some of the makrut basil sugar. You don't want to drown the dessert – 1–2 teaspoons of sugar will do. Top with finger lime pearls and serve.

Lemon curd

Burnt butter, bay leaf and lemon curd blondies

I love the contrast of the bay leaf with the sweet tartness of the lemon here. There is an aromatic taste of earth that tempers the sweetness perfectly. Just be sure to brown your butter right to the edge, as it grounds all the flavours, improved only by the smallest sprinkling of salt. **Serves 8**

200 g (7 oz) unsalted butter

4–6 bay leaves

320 g (11½ oz) light brown sugar

2 large free-range organic eggs

1 generous tablespoon vanilla bean paste

200 g (7 oz) plain (all-purpose) flour

150 g (5½ oz) coarsely chopped couverture white chocolate

125–185 ml (4–6 fl oz/½–¾ cup) Lemon curd (page 151)

Preheat the oven to 180°C (360°F). Generously grease and line a 20 cm (8 in) square baking tin with baking paper, allowing a generous overhang for easy lifting when it is ready.

Add the butter and half the bay leaves to a saucepan over medium heat. Stir often as the butter melts. Once melted, cook, swilling the pan often but not stirring, until a deep amber-hued liquid is achieved. It will foam and hiss, but this subsides and indicates it is nearly done. Place a sieve over a large bowl and strain the butter mixture, discarding the leaves. Scrape any burnt bits that have formed in the pan into your butter mixture, then add the sugar, stirring to combine. Allow to cool, then whisk in the eggs and vanilla bean paste. Using a rubber spatula, fold through the flour, then the chopped chocolate.

Scrape the mixture into the tin and level the top with your spatula. Dollop in spoonfuls of lemon curd – you don't want to drown it, just a few generous dollops here and there. Scatter over the remaining bay leaves and a sprinkle of salt.

Bake for 30 minutes, until golden, crackled and shiny. The edges should be firm and the middle just set but with that glorious slightly gooey centre. Allow to cool completely in the tin before lifting out and slicing into generous squares.

Remove the leaves before eating.

If you have any left over (unlikely), it will keep, covered, on your counter for up to 3 days.

Lemon curd

Summer almond loaf cake with lemon curd, ricotta and blackberries

This wants to be sturdy, like a pound cake, but is actually soft and vulnerable, barely holding itself together. Cut into thick wedges, not elegant fine slices. This is not a cake for the dainty. **Serves 6–8**

180 g (6½ oz/1¾ cups) ground almonds

75 g (2¾ oz/½ cup) plain (all-purpose) flour

½ tablespoon baking powder

1 teaspoon ground cinnamon

200 g (7 oz) unsalted butter, at room temperature

165 g (6 oz/¾ cup) caster (superfine) sugar

55 g (2 oz/¼ cup, firmly packed) brown sugar

3 large organic free-range eggs

2 teaspoons vanilla bean paste

zest of 1 unwaxed lemon

250 g (9 oz) blackberries

125 g (4½ oz/½ cup) firm ricotta

250 ml (8½ fl oz/1 cup) Lemon curd (page 151)

icing (confectioners') sugar, to dust

Preheat the oven to 180°C (360°F). Grease and line a 21 × 11 × 7 cm (8¼ × 4¼ × 2¾ in) loaf (bar) tin with baking paper and leave an overhang on each side so you can easily remove the cake.

Whisk together the ground almonds, flour, baking powder, cinnamon and a pinch of salt.

In the bowl of a stand mixer fitted with the paddle attachment, beat the butter and both sugars on medium speed until light and fluffy, about 5 minutes – please don't rush this step. Fluffy, magic crumb-creating glory happens here.

Scrape down the bowl. Add the eggs, one at a time, beating well after each addition, then mix in the vanilla and lemon zest. Reduce the speed to low and add the flour mixture. Beat until a uniform and light batter has been achieved – don't beat for more than a few minutes. Fold half the blackberries through and dollop the ricotta and 3 tablespoons of the lemon curd in – you don't want to mix this through, rough lumps and bumps and blobs is what we want here.

Scrape into the prepared tin and dollop about half the remaining lemon curd over the top of the batter. Bake in the oven for about 50 minutes or until a skewer inserted into the middle comes out not clean, but with a few moist crumbs attached. Let cool in the tin for a good 15–20 minutes before gently lifting the cake out and transferring to a wire rack to cool. Top with the remaining lemon curd and a scattering of the remaining blackberries. Dust with icing sugar to finish.

Do not leave any behind.

Potato brioche doughnuts with lemon curd and vanilla crème fraîche

The combination of potato, the buttery goodness of a brioche dough and the overnight rise give this doughnut a brilliantly rich flavour and a touch of chew. Combined with the vanilla crème fraîche and the tang of curd, this is hand-held heaven. You will need to begin this recipe one day ahead. **Makes approximately 10 doughnuts**

Doughnuts

130 g (4½ oz) all-purpose potato, peeled and chopped into chunks

210 ml (7 fl oz) milk

1 teaspoon vanilla bean paste

55 g (2 oz/¼ cup) caster (superfine) sugar

1 × 7 g (¼ oz) sachet dried yeast

1 large organic free-range egg

1 tablespoon vanilla bean paste

400 g (14 oz) strong flour, plus extra for dusting

pinch of salt

60 g (2 oz) unsalted butter, cool and pliable, cut into very small cubes

cooking oil spray

approx. 1–1.5 litres (34–51 fl oz/ 4–6 cups) flavourless oil, for frying

snow sugar or caster (superfine) sugar, for dusting

250 ml (8½ fl oz/1 cup) Lemon curd (page 151)

Vanilla crème fraîche

125 g (4½ oz) crème fraîche

1 teaspoon vanilla bean paste

For the doughnuts, add the potato, milk and 150 ml (5 fl oz) water to a saucepan. Bring to a simmer and cook until the potato is soft and falling apart. Turn off the heat, add the vanilla and set aside to cool. Strain, reserving the liquid. Add 150 ml (5 fl oz) of the liquid (basically all of it) to the bowl of a stand mixer with the caster sugar and the yeast. Set aside until it appears foamy on the surface. Add the crushed potato, egg and tablespoon of vanilla, then tip the flour and salt in. Using the dough hook attachment, knead on low for 10 minutes or until the dough is soft and sticky. Add the butter, one piece at a time until incorporated; the dough should be shiny and smooth.

Remove the dough from the mixer, spray with the cooking oil spray and cover with plastic wrap. Let rest for 30 minutes.

Turn the dough out onto a lightly floured work surface and press out to a rough rectangle. Place the dough in a large container (at least 2.5 litre/85 fl oz capacity), spray lightly again with oil, cover and place in the fridge overnight.

The next day, roll the dough out to about 2.5 cm (1 in) thick. Using an 8 cm (3¼ in) round cutter, stamp out rings and place on a greased tray. Repeat with the remaining dough. Spray with oil and cover with plastic wrap. Set aside in a warm spot for about 1 hour – test by pushing your finger into the dough – it should dent and not bounce back.

Heat the oil in a deep-fryer or deep-frying pan to 180°C (360°F). Using a slotted spoon, lower the doughnuts into the oil, a few at a time and cook for about 1½ minutes each side or until pale golden. Remove with a slotted spoon and place on a wire rack over a tray. Allow the doughnuts to cool slightly before dusting with the snow sugar.

For the vanilla crème fraîche, combine the crème fraîche and vanilla in a bowl and set aside, covered, until ready to pipe.

Transfer the lemon curd and vanilla crème fraîche to separate piping (icing) bags fitted with a medium nozzle. Gently make an incision into the side of a doughnut, about halfway into the centre, and gently squeeze in the curd and then the vanilla crème fraîche. Repeat with the remaining doughnuts, crème fraîche and curd.

Best eaten the day they are made.

Lemon meringue and raspberry tart

I love how this showcases Lemon curd in all its sweet, mouth-puckering glory. It's bright, tart and citric with a soothing, buttery-sweet finish – a complete showstopper. Should you feel the need to use a store-bought sweet shortcrust pastry, I commend you. I have simply included the pastry-making details here because, for some of us, we need the therapy of kneading and resting dough. This is a completely personal (time-dependent) choice. **Serves 8–10**

500 g (1 lb 2 oz/2 cups) Lemon curd (page 151)

1½ titanium-strength gelatine leaves

Pastry

250 g (9 oz) unsalted butter, chilled and cut into 1.5 cm (½ in) cubes

130 g (4½ oz/1 cup) icing (confectioners') sugar

2 teaspoons salt

40 g (1½ oz) organic free-range egg yolks (about 3 large)

330 g (11½ oz) plain (all purpose) flour

Preheat the oven to 180°C (360°F).

For the pastry, put the butter, icing sugar and salt in a bowl and mix well to combine. Add the egg yolks, one at a time, until incorporated. Fold through the flour until just combined. Turn out onto a clean work surface and gather together. Knead until the ingredients are incorporated. Shape the pastry into a round, flat disc. Cover and refrigerate for at least 2 hours (or freeze for future use).

Remove the pastry disc from the fridge 20 minutes before using. Roll the pastry between two sheets of baking paper until 3 mm (⅛ in) thick. Place on trays and refrigerate again for at least 20 minutes.

Grease and line a rectangular flan (tart) tin. Gently place the rolled pastry over the top and push it into the tin, trimming the sides. Pop the tin in the fridge for 20 minutes.

Remove the tin from the fridge, top the pastry with baking paper, then fill with pastry weights or uncooked rice. Blind bake for 20–25 minutes or until golden around the edges. Remove the weights or rice and return the pastry to the oven for a further 10 minutes – it should have a lovely tanned appearance. Remove from the oven and allow to cool.

Place the gelatine sheets in a bowl of iced water to bloom. While they are softening, place a saucepan over low heat. Add the curd and begin to warm it – you don't want to cook it, you just want to warm it enough to dissolve the gelatine. Once warm, add the bloomed gelatine and whisk until the gelatine is fully incorporated.

Carefully pour the curd into the cooked, cooled pastry shell and smooth the top using the back of a spoon. Place in the fridge for 30–45 minutes or until completely cooled and just set – it should

Cardamom raspberry layer

150 g (5½ oz) fresh raspberries

1 teaspoon vanilla bean paste

1 teaspoon ground cardamom

Italian meringue

330 g (11½ oz) caster (superfine) sugar

5 organic free-range egg whites

To top

Freeze-dried berries

Milk chocolate crisp pearls

Micro basil leaves, to scatter

be wobbly and slightly softer than a panna cotta in consistency.

For the cardamom raspberry layer, mash the raspberries, vanilla bean paste and cardamom in a bowl with a fork until the juices are released. Gently spread the raspberry mixture over the lemon curd.

For the Italian meringue, place the sugar in a heavy-based saucepan, add 60 ml (¼ cup) water and stir over low heat until the sugar dissolves. Increase the heat to high and cook until the syrup reaches 115°C (240°F) on a sugar thermometer, then remove from the heat.

Meanwhile, using an electric mixer, whisk the egg whites until soft peaks form, then, with the motor running, slowly pour in the hot sugar syrup in a steady stream and whisk for 5 minutes or until the bowl no longer feels warm to the touch. Reduce the speed to low and mix until the meringue reaches room temperature.

Scoop the meringue mixture onto the pie and gently use your spoon to create peaks and troughs – the less uniform, the better – as it helps to catch the flame when you torch it.

Use a blowtorch to toast the meringue until golden (optional). Scatter with the toppings and serve.

Slab of pav with elderflower gin cucumbers and lemon curd

The prettiest of desserts. Curd is done. Pav can be done ahead, and it helps to give the cucumbers a lovely little swim in the gin a good 30 minutes before serving. That just leaves assembly when it really counts. I make this with and without the crème fraîche component. There is enough going on that its inclusion isn't absolute. Play around with it and see what you prefer.
Serves 6

1 telegraph (long) cucumber, cut into strips using a vegetable peeler

60–125 ml (2–4 fl oz/¼–½ cup) aromatic or floral gin, as needed

2 tablespoons elderflower cordial

500 ml (17 fl oz/2 cups) Lemon curd (page 151)

200 g (7 oz) crème fraîche (optional)

elderflowers and edible flowers, to scatter

micro basil leaves (optional)

Pavlova

8 organic free-range egg whites, at room temperature

500 g (1 lb 2 oz) caster (superfine) sugar

1 tablespoon white wine vinegar

1 vanilla bean, seeds scraped (or 1 tablespoon vanilla bean paste)

Preheat the oven to 130°C (265°F). Line a large baking tray (approx. 40 x 30 cm/16 x 12 in) with baking paper.

For the pavlova, whisk the egg whites and a pinch of salt with an electric mixer to soft peaks, 4–5 minutes, then, with the motor running, gradually add the sugar and whisk until firm and glossy, 2–3 minutes. Rub some of the mixture between two fingers. If it feels grainy, continue mixing. You want to ensure you can't feel any sugar like sand. Once smooth, whisk in the vinegar and vanilla.

Turn the mixture out onto the prepared tray and, using a palette knife or spatula, spread the mixture across the baking paper, creating a few tips and dips in the meringue as you go.

Place in the oven, reduce the temperature to 120°C (235°F), and bake until crisp but not coloured, 1¼–1½ hours. Turn off the heat and leave to cool completely in the oven.

(You can store this in an airtight container for a day or so.)

Place the cucumber strips, 60 ml (2 fl oz/¼ cup) of gin and the elderflower cordial in a bowl. You want the cucumber to be touched by gin but not drowning in it. If you feel there isn't enough to adequately coat, add a little more, a splash at a time until the cucumber has been blessed by the gin. Let sit for about 15 minutes.

To plate, gently transfer your meringue to a serving platter. Scoop over the curd and the crème fraîche, if using. Strain the cucumbers from the gin bath, then place them on top of the pav slab. Add all the elderflower and edible flowers. Some micro basil is also lovely here.

Green goddess dressing

Green goddess and broccolini with sunflower seed dukkah 169

Green goddess, crushed peas, burrata and black olives 170

Saucy thighs 173

Sorta crispy chickpeas, green goddess and feta 175

 ## Tahini yoghurt dressing

Sticky eggplant on tahini yoghurt with pomegranate, chilli and pistachio 178

Roasted pumpkin and pickled onion salad with tahini yoghurt dressing 181

Roasted sweet potato and lentil salad with fried shallots, soft herbs and tahini yoghurt 182

Loaded falafel fries for when you need to let them feed themselves 183

Spicy roasted cauliflower with herbs, pomegranate and chickpeas 184

Tahini yoghurt salmon with puffed grain dukkah 187

 ## Thai-style dressing

Thai-inspired beef sub 190

Soba, seeds and sauce 191

Last-minute laarb of sorts 192

Poached chicken, herb and persimmon salad 194

Crunchy cukes with spicy peanut kinda nahm jim 196

Holy sh*t porchetta 199

 ## Ultimate ranch dressing

Cavolo nero, chorizo, preserved lemon with smoked almonds and ranch 202

Bloody Mary and parmesan tornado ta tas 204

Broccolini, freekeh and mint salad with ranch and pistachios 207

Sunday slow-roasted pastrami brisket with ranch, pickles and kettles 208

Crisp chicken, radish pea salad and ranch 210

Dressed for it

I have never been one to buy into the 'dressed for success' sentiment, unless it's related to food. Well-dressed food is going places. I love how a good dressing can puddle in the bottom of the bowl, begging to be swiped at or given a second life by a hunk of bread. A decent dressing can exert a mercurial forcefield on the blandest, most basic of ingredients, giving your midweek fuel some much needed mouth to mouth. The following dressings – a mix of tart, spicy, creamy and a touch sweet – do just that. I do have one rule when it comes to dressings. Remember they are there to enliven, not drench, the food they are served with. Use with a lightness of touch and your dinner will be rewarded.

Green goddess dressing

This dressing is fresh, vibrant and my kind of add-on to almost every meal. I know many iterations have been around the traps but, in terms of versatility, it was a must-include in the book. I've kept this vegan, but if you are chasing a bolder umami hit simply add three anchovies with the initial ingredients and continue with the recipe as normal.

To make 750 ml

(25½ fl oz/3 cups)

½ bunch coriander (cilantro), rinsed and chopped

1 bunch flat-leaf (Italian) parsley, washed, dried and chopped

½ bunch spring onions (scallions), green parts only, washed, dried and chopped

1 avocado

½ tbsp onion powder

½ tbsp ground coriander

2 small cloves smoked garlic

25 ml (¾ fl oz) lemon juice (juice of ½ large lemon)

200 ml (7 fl oz) water

salt

pinch of caster (superfine) sugar

½ tbsp honey mustard

150 ml (5 fl oz) olive oil

5 tsp apple cider vinegar

To make 1.5 litres

(51 fl oz/6 cups)

1 bunch coriander (cilantro), rinsed and chopped

2 bunches flat-leaf (Italian) parsley, washed, dried and chopped

1 bunch spring onions (scallions), green parts only, washed, dried and chopped

2 avocados

1 tbsp onion powder

1 tbsp ground coriander

3 cloves smoked garlic

50 ml (1¾ fl oz) lemon juice (juice of 1 large lemon)

400 ml (13½ fl oz) water

salt

½ tbsp caster (superfine) sugar

1 tbsp honey mustard

300 ml (10 fl oz) olive oil

50 ml (1¾ fl oz) apple cider vinegar

To make 2.25 litres

(76 fl oz/9 cups)

1½ bunches coriander (cilantro), rinsed and chopped

3 bunches flat-leaf (Italian) parsley, washed, dried and chopped

1½ bunches spring onions (scallions), green parts only, washed, dried and chopped

3 avocados

1½ tbsp onion powder

1½ tbsp ground coriander

5 small cloves smoked garlic

75 ml (2½ fl oz) lemon juice (juice of 1 large lemon)

600 ml (20½ fl oz) water

salt

¾ tbsp caster (superfine) sugar

1½ tbsp honey mustard

450 ml (15 fl oz) olive oil

75 ml (2½ fl oz) apple cider vinegar

Add the chopped herbs, avocado, spices, garlic, lemon juice, water, sugar and mustard to a blender. Blitz on high until everything is looking properly blitzed – depending on the power of your blender this can take a fair bit of whizzing. Once incorporated, add the olive oil and apple cider vinegar and blitz again – this will emulsify the dressing and stop it from splitting. It should be a vibrant green and seem a little aerated. Season generously with salt and freshly ground black pepper. Keeps, covered, in the fridge for 1 week.

Green goddess and broccolini with sunflower seed dukkah

Green, crunch, chew, colour. This is on my 'last-meal requests' shortlist. It's so quick to chuck together and you feel more and more virtuous with each bite. This recipe loves to hit the road with a bit of grilled chicken or roasted pumpkin (squash). I've even thrown a tin of smoked tuna in oil at it and called it a meal. **Serves 4 as part of a shared meal**

250 ml (8½ fl oz/1 cup) Green goddess dressing (page 166)

1–2 bunches broccolini

1 tablespoon olive oil

Dukkah

30 g (1 oz) sunflower seeds

1½ teaspoons urfa chilli flakes

1½ teaspoons aleppo pepper

pinch of ground turmeric

¼ teaspoon caster (superfine) sugar

Preheat the oven to 180°C (360°F).

Let the green goddess dressing sit on the bench while you prepare everything so it's not fridge-cold at serving.

For the dukkah, add the ingredients to a mortar and pestle. Give it one or two grinds – just to break up the sunflower seeds a little to release the oils and to ensure the ingredients are incorporated. Set aside.

Add the broccolini to a baking tray and drizzle with the olive oil. Season generously with salt and freshly ground black pepper, then toss to coat. Pop in the oven for 10 minutes. You want to give this a warm-up rather than a complete cook-through – just enough to get the flavours waking up while retaining excellent crunch and some freshness.

Pour the green goddess onto a serving plate. Top with the broccolini, scatter the dukkah over the top, then serve.

Green goddess, crushed peas, burrata and black olives

Dear peas,

I am sorry. So sorry for the years of shade I threw at you. The hours spent at the table staring you down with venom. I am sorry I tried to house you in my napkin and later feed you to my cat. (I also apologise to my cat.) I hope this dish makes up for my disrespectful pea-hating past. Much love, K.

This recipe is a riff on an Alison Roman favourite of mine, the Green goddess giving so much glorious lift and oomph to the pea, cheese and olive action.
Serves 6

65 g (2¼ oz) pitted black olives, finely chopped (or use 55 g/ 2 oz Olive tapenade on page 89, if you happen to have some stashed)

80 ml (2½ fl oz/⅓ cup) olive oil

zest and juice of 1 unwaxed lemon

310 g (11 oz/2 cups) peas (frozen is fine)

1 cup spicy greens (rocket/ arugula, flat-leaf/Italian parsley, mustard leaves)

250 ml (8½ fl oz/1 cup) Green goddess dressing (page 166)

1 ball burrata (150 g/5½ oz), drained

oregano leaves, to scatter

Combine the olives, olive oil and lemon zest in a bowl and set aside.

Using your hands, roughly pulp half the peas. You don't want purée here; you just want to rough them up a little.

Add the spicy greens, remaining whole peas and lemon juice to a bowl and toss to combine.

Add the green goddess to the base of a serving platter. Tear the burrata into pieces and scatter it over the green goddess. Spoon the olives, lemon zest and oil over. Top with the hand-crushed peas, then the remaining pea and greens mixture. Scatter with oregano leaves, season very generously with salt and freshly ground black pepper and serve.

Saucy thighs

Here, some chicken thighs are given a quick bath in Green goddess dressing; barbecued until charred, tanned and golden; then brought to a plate with even more Green goddess and all the green, crisp things you can find. It's marvellous, easy, dinnertime glory. **Serves 4–6**

5–6 boneless, skinless chicken thighs

375 ml (12½ fl oz/1½ cups) Green goddess dressing (page 166)

3 tablespoons olive oil, for drizzling, plus extra to serve

1 bunch rocket (arugula) (the milder less bitter/peppery leaf works best here)

1 cup mixed fresh herbs – I used flat-leaf (Italian) parsley, fennel, coriander (cilantro) and basil

any lettuce leaves and bits and bobs to dress this work well

lemon cheeks and olive oil, to dress

Add the chicken thighs and 250 ml (1 cup) of the green goddess to a bowl. Stab the chicken with a bit of reserved rage here and there to puncture a few spots to help the marinade penetrate. Toss to coat then let it sit on your kitchen bench for 20 minutes.

Heat a barbecue or chargrill pan to medium-high. Drizzle the chicken with oil and grill until browned and cooked through, 8-10 minutes.

Meanwhile, add the remaining green goddess to the base of a serving plate. Top with your herbs, lettuce leaves and bits and bobs. Top with the chicken, then dress with lemon cheeks and olive oil. Season with salt and freshly ground black pepper and serve.

Green goddess dressing

Sorta crispy chickpeas, green goddess and feta

The ease of this dish – the throw-it-on carefree nature, and sensational taste of it – proves we can be less uptight about dinner and far better fed. It's an absolute 2-minute dinner winner. **Serves 6**

310 ml (10½ fl oz/1¼ cups) Green goddess dressing (page 166)

125 ml (4 fl oz/½ cup) olive oil, plus extra to drizzle

1 onion, thinly sliced

850 g (1 lb 14 oz) tinned chickpeas, rinsed thoroughly and drained

2 garlic cloves, smashed

1 tablespoon aleppo pepper, plus extra to serve

120 g (4½ oz) crumbled Persian feta

1 cup soft herbs (I used dill and basil, but whatever you have on hand always seems to work with this)

Let the green goddess dressing sit on the bench while you prepare everything so it's not fridge-cold at serving.

Heat the oil in a frying pan over medium heat. Add the onion and cook, stirring often, until it is lovely and soft and only just starting to colour, about 8 minutes. Add the chickpeas, garlic and aleppo pepper and toss gently to coat everything in the onion and oil mixture. Keep cooking, giving the pan a jiggle here and there to prevent burning and to ensure your chickpeas are getting an equal time tanning in the pan. They should look a little caramelised and crisp (ish) in spots. When done, remove from the heat and add the herbs and quickly stir to combine.

Add the green goddess to a serving plate. Spoon over the chickpea mixture and give everything a lovely heave of salt and freshly ground black pepper – and another pinch of aleppo pepper for good measure.

Top with the feta pieces and herbs and scatter over a pinch or so more of aleppo pepper. Drizzle over some olive oil, season again and serve.

Tahini yoghurt dressing

I love a good yoghurt dressing. It offers richness and acidity and unlike so many dressings, can be devoid of sweetness, which often allows the ingredients it dresses to shine more brightly. Here, unsweetened yoghurt offers a glorious shudder of freshness, which contrasts with the rounded creaminess of the tahini. The pragmatic and the romantic working together for one of the easiest, most useful dressings you should have in your repertoire. It tap dances its way to the table every single time.

To make 250 ml
(8½ fl oz/1 cup)

185 g (6½ oz/¾ cup) thick
   Greek-style yoghurt
2 tbsp hulled tahini
juice of ½ lemon
1 tbsp extra-virgin olive oil
½ garlic clove, finely grated
pinch of finely ground cumin

To make 500 ml
(17 fl oz/2 cups)

370 g (13 oz/1½ cups) thick
   Greek-style yoghurt
4 tbsp hulled tahini
juice of 1 lemon
2 tbsp extra-virgin olive oil
1 garlic clove, finely grated
1 tsp finely ground cumin

To make 750 ml
(25½ fl oz/3 cups)

555 g (1 lb 4 oz/3 cups) thick
   Greek-style yoghurt
6 tbsp hulled tahini
juice of 1½ lemons
3 tbsp extra-virgin olive oil
1½ garlic cloves, finely grated
2 tsp finely ground cumin

Optional extra: ¼ cup coriander (cilantro) leaves, finely chopped per 250 ml (1 cup) of dressing

Combine all the ingredients in a bowl and whisk vigorously until fully incorporated.
Taste and adjust seasoning with salt, lemon juice and freshly ground black pepper. Keeps in the fridge for up to 2 weeks in a tightly sealed jar.

Sticky eggplant on tahini yoghurt with pomegranate, chilli and pistachio

The eggplant (aubergine) gets a double dressing here. Charred until black and soft, then slathered in a date paste and caramelised briefly in the oven, it's a spectacular meal with flatbread on the side for necessary mopping. I've left the eggplant skin on here, which I know divides people. I love the crunch and smokiness but if you prefer the skin off, peel after roasting and carefully transfer the 'naked' plant to the serving plate and place on top of the tahini yoghurt. **Serves 2–4**

2 eggplants (aubergines), washed thoroughly

375 ml (12½ fl oz/1½ cups) Tahini yoghurt dressing (page 177)

1 green chilli, thinly sliced

½ cup mint leaves, loosely packed, coarsely torn

65 g (2¼ oz) roughly chopped pistachio kernels

4 tablespoons pomegranate arils

Quick date paste of sorts

135 g (5 oz) dried medjool dates, pitted

boiling water

2 tablespoons pomegranate molasses

2 tablespoons olive oil

For the quick date paste, add the dates to a bowl and cover in boiling water. Soak until soft, about 15 minutes. Transfer to a blender with the remaining paste ingredients and blitz until you get a chunky jam consistency. Scoop into a bowl, season with salt and freshly ground black pepper and set aside.

Preheat the oven to 175°C (345°F). Line a baking tray with baking paper. Preheat a barbecue grill until hot.

Add the eggplants to the barbecue plate and let the fire do its thing. Turn the eggplants regularly so they char all over. You want them to get black, even white in a few places, about 15–20 minutes. You can achieve a similar result by roasting in an oven at 200°C (390°F), turning regularly.

Carefully transfer the eggplants to the prepared tray. Cut down the centre of the eggplants to fan them out slightly. Dollop the date paste across the open flesh, season with salt and pepper and roast in the oven for 15–20 minutes.

Smear the base of a large serving plate with the tahini yoghurt dressing. Carefully place the eggplants on top of the yoghurt. Don't worry about any of the date mixture falling onto the yoghurt, this only adds to the flavour. Top with the chilli, mint leaves, pistachio kernels and pomegranate arils and serve.

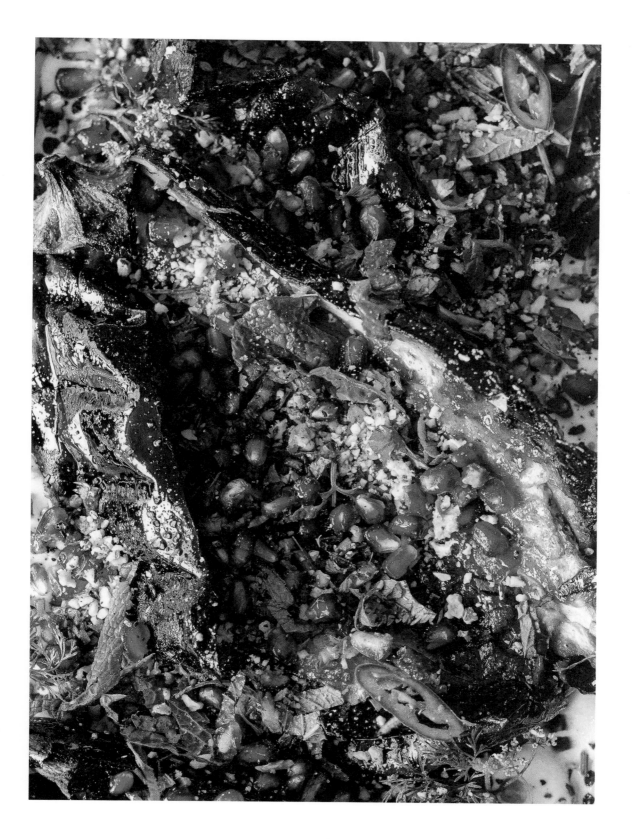

Tahini yoghurt dressing

Roasted pumpkin and pickled onion salad with tahini yoghurt dressing

This is a salad of contrasts. Bitter crunchy leaves meet sweet, melting, caramelised pumpkin. The crunch of pepitas and chickpeas are tempered by the herby, creamy Tahini yoghurt dressing. The refreshing tartness of pickled onion is countered by a scattering of chopped dates. It's my kind of salad. Robust, hearty, textured and colourful. **Serves 4**

1 kg (2 lb 3 oz) Japanese pumpkin, skin on, cut into even-sized wedges

3 tablespoons olive oil, plus extra to serve

2 tablespoons maple syrup

1 radicchio, trimmed, leaves gently torn

8 medium cavolo nero (Tuscan kale) leaves, stems removed, roughly shredded

400 g (14 oz) tinned chickpeas, rinsed thoroughly and drained

4–6 dates, roughly chopped

2–3 tablespoons pepitas (pumpkin seeds), lightly toasted in a dry pan until fragrant

185 ml (6 fl oz/¾ cup) Tahini yoghurt dressing (page 177)

Quick pickled onions

1 red onion, thinly sliced into half moons

125 ml (4 fl oz/½ cup) apple cider vinegar

1 tablespoon salt

1 tablespoon caster (superfine) sugar

For the quick pickled onions, add all the ingredients to a bowl, give them a gentle stir and set aside. You just want some of that strong bite to subside and, once the onion has softened a little, you can be confident they are good to go – about 20 minutes should do it.

Preheat the oven to 175°C (345°F).

Add the pumpkin wedges to a baking tray. Drizzle with the olive oil and maple syrup and turn to coat. Season generously with salt and freshly ground black pepper. Roast for about 40 minutes, or until the pumpkin is caramelised on top and cooked through. Allow to cool slightly – this is lovely served when the pumpkin is warm.

Spread the radicchio and cavolo nero leaves across a serving platter and scatter over the chickpeas. Add the pumpkin pieces, then scatter the pickled onions and dates on top. Drizzle with the tahini dressing, top with the pepitas and finish with an extra drizzle of olive oil. Season generously with salt and pepper and serve.

Roasted sweet potato and lentil salad with fried shallots, soft herbs and tahini yoghurt

Earthy flavours upon earthy flavours, this whole thing is a vibe. Don't skimp on the frying part of the shallots – it takes the salad to the places you really want to go. **Serves 4**

3 sweet potatoes, peeled and chopped into even-sized cubes

5 tablespoons olive oil

110 g (4 oz) Puy lentils

3–4 French shallots, peeled, halved lengthways and thinly sliced

½ cup mint leaves, chopped

½ cup coriander (cilantro) leaves, chopped

4 cups loosely packed English spinach leaves

125–185 ml (½–¾ cup) Tahini yoghurt dressing (page 177)

2 teaspoons sumac, to scatter

Preheat the oven to 180°C (360°F). Line a large roasting tray with baking paper.

Place the sweet potato on the prepared tray, drizzle with 3 tablespoons of the olive oil and, using your hands, toss to coat the potato in the oil. Season generously with salt and freshly ground black pepper. Pop in the oven and roast until the sweet potato has cooked through and caramelised on the edges but still retaining some shape, about 45 minutes.

Cook the lentils in a saucepan of boiling water until tender, 20–25 minutes, then drain, refresh and drain again well. Season immediately with salt and pepper and 1 tablespoon of olive oil, turning them to coat. Set aside.

While the potato and lentils are cooking, place a small frying pan over medium–high heat. Add the remaining oil and, once shimmering, fry the shallots until crisp and golden and charred in spots – this is where the depth of the flavour is so don't be afraid to let it take on quite a bit of colour. Drain on paper towel.

To serve, add the sweet potato to a bowl with the herbs, lentils and spinach and toss gently to combine. Turn out onto a serving plate and drizzle with the tahini yoghurt dressing. Sprinkle with sumac, then top with a pile of the fried shallots. Season again with salt and pepper and serve.

Loaded falafel fries for when you need to let them feed themselves

Some days, plates and cutlery are overrated. This is a recipe for those days. The 'can't cook but can assemble' days. The 'I don't even want Uber Eats' days. These are the days that motivated this very book – take a premade dressing and some fridge fodder and, voila, you have a meal. It's planning without the commitment, yet with all the flavour. **Serves 4**

800 g (1 lb 12 oz) all-purpose potatoes, peeled, cut lengthways into even-sized chips (or substitute with a 750 g/ 1 lb 11 oz bag of store-bought frozen chips/fries)

4–5 tablespoons olive oil

3 falafels (feel free to make your own here)

½ cup each chopped flat-leaf (Italian) parsley, coriander (cilantro), mint and dill

3–4 radishes, thinly sliced

500 g (1 lb 2 oz) medley cherry tomatoes, quartered

4 tablespoons za'atar, or to taste

185 ml (6 fl oz/¾ cup) Tahini yoghurt dressing (page 177) (well done, you already made this)

Preheat the oven 190°C (375°F). Line a large baking tray with baking paper.

Spread the chips in a single layer on the prepared tray, drizzle them with the olive oil and turn to coat. Season with salt and freshly ground black pepper. Roast in the oven until golden and crisp, about 40–50 minutes.

When you have about 15 minutes remaining of roasting time, add the falafels to the roasted potato tray. Cook in the oven for a further 15–20 minutes or until the chips are crisp and the falafels cooked through.

Pull the falafels from the oven and coarsely break them up into a bowl – you are wanting to create a kind of falafel crumble here. Season with salt and pepper then, once cooled slightly, add the herbs, radish slices and tomatoes. Gently toss to combine.

Pull the chips from the oven and immediately douse in za'atar. Plate them and top with the falafel and salad mixture and drizzle the tahini yoghurt dressing at will. Season again and serve immediately. Preferably straight from the tray.

Spicy roasted cauliflower with herbs, pomegranate and chickpeas

This is beyond surprisingly good. Like many a child of the 1980s I've got creamy baked cauliflower PTSD – that homogenous baked-into-oblivion dish that I thought had truly ruined the humble brassica for me forever. Enter this cauliflower replacement therapy. It's got texture, a heap of flavour and is a visual delight to bring to the table. Get involved. **Serves 4**

1 head of cauliflower, base trimmed

4 tablespoons olive oil

4 tablespoons Harissa (you should totally make the Harissa on page 79)

200 g (7 oz) tinned chickpeas, rinsed thoroughly and drained

1 tablespoon sumac

1 teaspoon brown sugar

375 ml (12½ fl oz/1½ cups) Tahini yoghurt dressing (page 177)

4 tablespoons pomegranate molasses

arils of 1 pomegranate

Trench coat of herbs

¼ cup dill fronds

½ cup basil leaves, coarsely torn

¾ cup flat-leaf (Italian) parsley, chopped

¾ cup coriander (cilantro) leaves, chopped

Fill a large saucepan with water and season with salt. Bring to the boil. Add the cauliflower and cook for 6–8 minutes, depending on the size. Check to see if it's ready by poking the stem with a knife – it should pierce the base with relative ease.

Remove the cauliflower and place on a baking tray and set aside to steam-dry for around 10 minutes.

Preheat the oven to 180°C (360°F).

Line the same tray with baking paper, then return the cauliflower to the tray. Rub the cauliflower with 3 tablespoons of the olive oil and the harissa. Roast, uncovered, for 45 minutes – the edges get super-crispy and charred, and the olive oil makes it almost buttery.

Add the chickpeas, sumac and brown sugar to a bowl with 1 tablespoon olive oil. Turn to coat. For the last 15 minutes of cooking, add the chickpeas to the cauliflower in the oven. Throw them around it and quickly close the oven door to let it keep doing its thing.

For the trench coat, combine the herbs in a bowl and set aside.

Remove the cauliflower from the oven and carefully transfer to a serving plate, scooping all the chickpeas and residual juices onto the plate. Pour the tahini yoghurt dressing over the top, drizzle with pomegranate molasses and season with salt and freshly ground black pepper. Cover with the trench coat of herbs and the pomegranate arils to finish. Serve as is at the table.

Tahini yoghurt dressing

Tahini yoghurt salmon with puffed grain dukkah

This recipe has got all your necessary touch points: the silky creamy fish, the hit of spice, the crunch and intrigue of the puffed grain dukkah. It's easy, looks great, tastes even better, and you've armed yourself with time by prepping 90 per cent of it in advance – the key to any happy dinner plans. Oh, and please take the time to source sustainably farmed salmon. **Serves 4**

1 × 500–700 g (1 lb 2 oz–1 lb 9 oz) approx. side of salmon

1 teaspoon olive oil

sea salt flakes

Marinade

6 tablespoons Tahini yoghurt dressing (page 177), plus extra to serve

1 small garlic clove, crushed

1 heaped tablespoon berber spice

1 teaspoon ground turmeric

1 teaspoon paprika

finely grated zest of 1 unwaxed lemon, plus juice of ½ lemon

Puffed grain dukkah

pinch of chilli flakes

pinch of lemon zest

1 tablespoon puffed quinoa

1 tablespoon pine nuts toasted in a dry pan until fragrant

2 tablespoons puffed amaranth

pinch of dried saltbush (omit if unavailable)

pinch of flaked sea salt (smoked if you have it)

¼ cup finely chopped coriander (cilantro) leaves

Preheat the oven to 125°C (255°F). Line a baking tray with baking paper.

To make the puffed grain dukkah, simply combine all the ingredients in a bowl and set aside.

Add all the marinade ingredients to a bowl large enough to hold the salmon. Add the salmon and gently turn to coat, rubbing the yoghurt mixture into the fish. Drizzle with the olive oil and salt flakes. Gently transfer the fish to the prepared tray and drizzle over a little olive oil. Cook in the oven for 15–17 minutes, or until cooked to your liking. I always like to check as time will vary depending on the thickness of the piece of fish.

Remove the fish from the oven and immediately press the dukkah mixture onto the surface of the fish. Sprinkle over a few pomegranate arils, season with salt and freshly ground black pepper and serve with the extra tahini yoghurt dressing on the side.

To serve

pomegranate arils, to scatter

Tahini yoghurt dressing

Thai-style dressing

This dressing is bold, exciting and I could eat it on almost anything. You might want to drink it, so I suggest you protect your shirt in advance. It can play marinade as well as dressing and gives the blandest of foods vital, life-affirming spark. In other words: it's a dinnertime essential. I've given a giant quantity of 4.5 litres (18 cups) in case you also want to move this into a gift category and make lifelong friends.

To make 1.5 litres
(51 fl oz/6 cups)

500 ml (17 fl oz/2 cups) sweet chilli sauce

250 ml (8½ fl oz/1 cup) kecap manis

100 ml (3½ fl oz) fish sauce

½ tbsp sesame oil

250 ml (8½ fl oz/1 cup) vegetable oil

250 ml (8½ fl oz/1 cup) lemon juice

50 ml (1¾ fl oz) mirin

½ thumb-sized piece of fresh ginger, peeled and chopped

½ thumb-sized piece of galangal, peeled and chopped

½ lemongrass stem, white part only, chopped

2 garlic cloves, chopped

½ cup Vietnamese mint leaves, chopped

½ large bunch coriander (cilantro), roots, stalks and leaves, rinsed

½ bunch mint, leaves picked, stalks discarded

6 makrut lime leaves, deveined and chopped

To make 3 litres
(101 fl oz/12 cups)

1 litre (34 fl oz/4 cups) sweet chilli sauce

500 ml (17 fl oz/2 cups) kecap manis

200 ml (7 fl oz) fish sauce

1 tbsp sesame oil

500 ml (17 fl oz/2 cups) vegetable oil

500 ml (17 fl oz/2 cups) lemon juice

100 ml (3½ fl oz) mirin

1 thumb-sized piece of fresh ginger, peeled and chopped

1 thumb-sized piece of galangal, peeled and chopped

1 lemongrass stem, white part only, chopped

4 garlic cloves, chopped

1 cup Vietnamese mint leaves, chopped

1 large bunch coriander (cilantro), roots, stalks and leaves, rinsed

1 bunch mint, leaves, picked, stalks discarded

12 makrut lime leaves, deveined and chopped

To make 4.5 litres
(152 fl oz/18 cups)

1.5 litres (51 fl oz/6 cups) sweet chilli sauce

750 ml (25½ fl oz/3 cups) kecap manis

300 ml (10 fl oz) fish sauce

2 tbsp sesame oil

750 ml (25½ fl oz/3 cups) vegetable oil

750 ml (25½ fl oz/3 cups) lemon juice

200 ml (7 fl oz) mirin

1½ thumb-sized piece of fresh ginger, peeled and chopped

1½ thumb-sized piece of galangal, peeled and chopped

1½ lemongrass stem, white part only, chopped

6 garlic cloves, chopped

1½ cups Vietnamese mint leaves, chopped

1½ large bunches coriander (cilantro), roots, stalks and leaves, rinsed

1½ bunches mint, leaves picked, stalks discarded

18 makrut lime leaves, deveined and chopped

Place all the ingredients in a food processor and whizz until smooth. The lemongrass can give this a slight furry element given how woody and fibrous it is. I love it, it makes me feel like I know what I am eating. However, if you prefer you can simply strain the dressing to catch any of the larger more fibrous elements.

This dressing can sit happily in the fridge in a screw-top jar for about 6 months although I promise you it's simply not going to last that long.

Thai-inspired beef sub

The quickest throw-together meal if ever there was one. If you are an epic forward planner (please teach me), then this is great in the following sequence. Make dressing. Double batch the meatballs. Freeze one lot. Eat the other. Your future self will thank you. **Serves 6–8**

600 g (1 lb 5 oz) ground (minced) beef

6 tablespoons Thai-style dressing (page 188)

2 tablespoons olive oil

Rolls

1–2 baguettes, halved horizontally, slightly warmed in the oven

Thai-style dressing (about 1½ tablespoons per serve), plus extra to drizzle

kewpie mayonnaise

1 carrot, peeled into ribbons

1 small Lebanese (short) cucumber, peeled into ribbons

Vietnamese mint

coriander (cilantro) leaves

1–2 radishes, thinly sliced

Preheat the oven to 180°C (360°F). Line a baking tray with baking paper.

Add the beef and Thai-style dressing to a bowl. Add a heft of salt and freshly ground black pepper and mix, using your hands to incorporate the dressing through the minced meat. Once fully incorporated, roll the mixture into meatballs, approximately the size of a golf ball. Place on the prepared tray.

Place an ovenproof non-stick frying pan over medium heat. Add the oil and, once hot, add the meatballs, searing them on all sides until brown and caramelised, 1–2 minutes. It's important to watch this step as the soy and sugars in the meatball mixture will caramelise them relatively quickly. You also want to let them cook relatively undisturbed for the first part of cooking so that they don't break apart when you try to turn them. I try to turn them only once when on the stovetop. Transfer the pan to the oven and roast for 8 minutes or until just cooked through.

While the meatballs are in the oven, prepare your baguettes. Smear the inside of the rolls with Thai-style dressing and kewpie mayonnaise. Layer the carrot, cucumber, Vietnamese mint, coriander and radish. Gently top with the meatballs and season with salt. Top with extra mayonnaise and Thai-style dressing and serve.

Soba, seeds and sauce

This is literally the extent of this 'throw in a bowl and call it a meal' mastery. In many ways this recipe is the epitome of this book. All the work is done, and in the sauce. Just throw some noods in boiling water and a meal is at the ready. If you want to add a bit of extra oomph, a fried or poached egg would be right at home here. **Serves 2**

270 g (9½ oz) soba noodles

250 ml (8½ fl oz/1 cup) Thai-style dressing (page 188)

30 g (1 oz/¼ cup) pepitas (pumpkin seeds), toasted in a dry pan until fragrant

30 g (1 oz/¼ cup) sunflower seeds, toasted in a dry pan until fragrant

1 cup mixed herbs (mint, coriander/ cilantro, Thai basil), chopped

red sorrel, to scatter (so completely optional)

Cook the noodles according to the packet instructions and immediately refresh under cold water. Transfer to a bowl, add the Thai-style dressing and stir gently to coat. Cover and pop in the fridge to cool completely. This is at its glorious best as a cold noodle salad.

When ready to serve, give the noodles 10 minutes sitting on the bench, then add the seeds and herbs. Using tongs, gently incorporate the seed and herb mixture through the noodles. Turn into serving bowls and scatter with red sorrel, if using.

Last-minute laarb of sorts

Meat salad is my kind of salad. I like to serve this with crisp rice-paper cups and lettuce. Just like tacos, no one should have to choose between soft and crisp options. I've included ground rice in this version which adds spectacular texture, but I understand toasting and grinding rice is not your average Tuesday-night dinner prep. Some Asian grocers and delis sell ground rice; ensure you aren't purchasing rice flour – not what you want here – or omit if not easily accessible. **Serves 4**

1 tablespoon flavourless oil

2 red Asian shallots thinly sliced

400 g (14 oz) minced (ground) chicken

1½ teaspoons fish sauce, plus extra

100 ml (3½ fl oz) Thai-style dressing (page 188), plus more to serve

1 tablespoon chopped lemongrass, white part only

2 makrut lime leaves, stem removed, thinly sliced

2 tablespoons ground rice

4–5 thin slices galangal

4 tablespoons lime juice

½ cup fried shallots

2 tablespoons sliced spring onions (scallions)

¼ cup coriander (cilantro) leaves plus extra to serve

¼ cup torn mint, plus extra to serve

sliced red chillies (optional)

Crisp rice paper

rice bran or flavourless oil

4–6 rice paper spring roll wrappers (Vietnamese-style, not spring roll pastry)

To make the crisp rice paper cups, place a large frying pan over high heat. Coat the base of the pan in oil – you want to have a thin film of oil as it seems to puff best like this. Once the oil is hot and shimmering, add a sheet of rice paper, pressing down on it with a pair of tongs as it puffs and moves around, until all the translucent parts have puffed white and golden in spots. Remove from the heat and set aside on a plate.

Repeat with the remaining rice paper sheets and additional oil, reapplying the oil for each rice sheet.

Return pan to medium heat. Add the oil and once hot, add the shallots and cook until translucent. Add the chicken and cook until browned. Add the fish sauce, Thai-style dressing, lemongrass, makrut leaves, ground rice and galangal and cook for another 2–3 minutes over high heat, stirring regularly to prevent catching. Remove from the heat and taste. Adjust the seasoning with fish sauce, lime juice and Thai-style dressing.

To finish, add fried shallots, spring onion and all the soft herbs and toss gently until evenly distributed. Taste and adjust the seasoning again; it should have all the hallmarks of a Thai salad: spicy, sour and salty with a rounded sweetness that should not dominate.

Top with extra sliced red chillies if you love the heat and serve with lettuce, crispy rice cups, extra herbs, lime wedges and more Thai-style dressing to finish.

To serve

additional Thai-style dressing (page 189)

1 cos (romaine) lettuce, leaves separated and washed

store-bought crispy-fried shallots

Thai-style dressing

Poached chicken, herb and persimmon salad

Poached chicken often reeks of insidious diet culture telling you to strip all the joy from the bird, badger it in a hot bath, and call it a meal. Not here. In this recipe, the thighs get a gentle coconut bath, before being shredded and tossed through a rainforest-worth of salad ingredients, some vermicelli for contrast and persimmon for sweetness. **Serves 4**

500 g (1 lb 2 oz) boneless, skinless chicken thighs

400 ml (13½ fl oz) chicken stock

400 ml (13½ fl oz) coconut milk

200 g (7 oz) dried rice vermicelli noodles

125 ml (4 fl oz/½ cup) Thai-style dressing (page 188), to serve

squeeze of lime juice, to dress

store-bought crispy-fried shallots, to serve

Salad

250 g (9 oz) cherry tomatoes, halved

1 telegraph (long) cucumber, sliced

1 bunch coriander (cilantro) leaves, rinsed

½ bunch mint, leaves picked

2 persimmons, shaved into ribbons using a peeler

½ small red onion, sliced

60 ml (2 fl oz/¼ cup) Thai-style dressing

To poach the chicken, add the chicken thighs, stock and coconut milk to a medium saucepan. Bring to the boil, then reduce the heat to low and simmer for 5–7 minutes. Remove from the heat and let the chicken cool in the poaching liquid.

Transfer the chicken to a bowl and shred using two forks. Season with salt, freshly ground black pepper and 2 tablespoons Thai dressing while the chicken is still warm.

Put the vermicelli in a large bowl and pour in enough boiling water to cover. Leave to soak for 10 minutes, or until the noodles are translucent and softened. Drain the vermicelli in a colander and rinse with cold water. Drain well.

Using scissors, cut the long noodle strands in half, then tip them into a large bowl. Add the salad ingredients and the shredded chicken and toss gently. Using tongs, try to mix the salad and chicken ingredients through the noodles.

Turn onto serving plates. Drizzle with the remaining Thai-style dressing, a squeeze of lime juice and a generous handful of fried shallots, then serve.

Thai-style dressing

Crunchy cukes with spicy peanut kinda nahm jim

This dish is a shock of contrasts. Sour and sweet, soft and crunch. Just the way I like it. Spectacular with some grilled fish. **Serves 4 as part of a shared meal**

4 Lebanese (short) cucumbers

Thai-style dressing (page 188), to serve

Dressing

1 small garlic clove, grated

1 tablespoon sake

1 tablespoon lemon juice

1½ tablespoons soy sauce

1 teaspoon grated fresh ginger

1 tablespoon black sesame seeds

½ tablespoon Thai-style dressing

Peanut nahm jim

100 g (3½ oz) caster (superfine) sugar

55 g (2 oz) roasted peanuts

3 tablespoons Thai-style dressing

1 garlic clove

1 large red chilli, deseeded

½ cup coriander (cilantro) leaves

1 makrut lime leaf, deveined and chopped

To make the peanut nahm jim, add the sugar and 3 tablespoons water to a saucepan and place over high heat. Cook for 2–3 minutes or until the sugar has completely dissolved and is taking on a dark caramel colour.

While the sugar is cooking, spread the peanuts on a baking tray lined with baking paper. As soon as the sugar has turned that golden colour, pour it over the peanuts on the tray. Allow it to cool slightly but not harden, then drizzle with the Thai dressing. You don't want to add the dressing so quickly that it burns from the hot sugar and takes on a sour taste, but you don't want to let the hot sugar cool so much that it sets before you add the dressing and all it does is sit on top. Wait until it looks as though it is taking on a sheen on the surface, then quickly drizzle with the dressing. Let stand until set and completely cooled, 10–15 minutes.

Combine the dressing ingredients in a bowl and stir to combine.

Cut the cucumbers into wedges and place on a serving plate. Spoon over the dressing – you want enough to just sit on the cucumbers, not drown them.

Add the peanut brittle, and remaining nahm jim ingredients to a blender and pulse briefly to combine. You want this to look like a crunchy sort of relish consistency. Spoon it over the cucumbers and serve with extra Thai-style dressing.

Thai-style dressing

197

Dressed for it

Holy sh*t porchetta

I feel like the title says it all. Crisp crackling, fragrant filling, the dressing to finish. File this under 'must make'. Right now. Or as soon as time permits.
Serves 8–12

2 kg (4 lb 6 oz) piece pork belly, skin on, room temperature (I always like to explain to the butcher that I am undertaking a porchetta, as often they will cut it specifically for you. Also ask for a piece that has been hanging – this will increase your crisp crackling action and give you a great head start)

125–185 ml (½–¾ cup) Thai-style dressing (page 188), to serve

coriander (cilantro) leaves, to scatter

Stuffing

1 large bunch coriander (cilantro), rinsed

2 large red chillies, deseeded and roughly chopped

50 g (1¾ oz) desiccated coconut

4 garlic cloves, peeled and roughly chopped

juice of 2 limes

2 tablespoons Thai-style dressing

2 makrut lime leaves, deveined

Place the pork, skin side down, on a board.

Add the stuffing ingredients to a blender and give it a quick blitz to a rough relish consistency. Rub the mixture on the inside of the pork belly, with the majority of the mixture running down through the centre.

Roll the pork belly lengthways and, using butcher's twine, tie the meat at 2.5 cm (1 in) intervals to hold it together. Don't go measuring this with a ruler – you want even and regular twine to ensure the roll stays intact during cooking.

Wipe with a clean cloth to remove the salt.

Preheat the oven to 220°C (430°F).

Place the porchetta on a rack inside a roasting tin. Roast in the oven for 20 minutes. Reduce the heat to 150°C (300°F) and cook for 2½–3 hours. Remove from the oven and leave to sit and rest for 15 minutes.

To serve, remove the string and cut the pork into thick slices using a serrated knife. Drizzle over some of the Thai-style dressing and scatter with coriander leaves. Season generously with salt and freshly ground black pepper.

Make sure you serve it with additional Thai-style dressing – people are going to want more.

Here are some simple rules for super crisp crackling:

- Air-dry. Let it hang about in your fridge, uncovered, for 2 days. Minimum.
- Score the rind, then salt. Rub her down like a swimmer with lard about to cross the English Channel.
- The initial temp needs to be blistering hot.
- Once cooked, leave the meat to stand away from the heat on a bench somewhere, nowhere near your mouth. Leave it for 10–20 minutes, uncovered. The juices, which have been driven to the centre of the meat during cooking, will then redistribute back through the meat, so that it loses less juice when you cut it and be more tender and juicier. No resting under foil here.

Ultimate ranch dressing

This wonderful ranch dressing adds a depth of flavour and lubrication to anything it touches. It traverses seasons with ease. It cools, refreshes, brightens, and adds heat with its bite of pungent horseradish – adjust to taste depending on whether you use freshly grated or cream. Ranch is such a universal pleasure; I've even caught my smallest child trying to drink it. No judgement: I'd probably take a Cleopatra-style bath in the stuff given the opportunity.

To make 375 ml
(13 fl oz/1½ cups)

125 ml (4 fl oz/½ cup) buttermilk

185 g (6½ oz/¾ cup) kewpie mayonnaise

1½ tbsp oyster sauce

1 tbsp horseradish (fresh grated or cream), or to taste

½ cup dill fronds, finely chopped

½ cup flat-leaf (Italian) parsley, finely chopped

To make 750 ml
(25½ fl oz/3 cups)

250 ml (8½ fl oz/1 cup) buttermilk

375 g (13 oz/1½ cups) kewpie mayonnaise

3 tbsp oyster sauce

2 tbsp horseradish (fresh grated or cream), or to taste

1 cup dill fronds, finely chopped

1 cup flat–leaf parsley, finely chopped

To make 1.5 litres
(51 fl oz/6 cups)

500 ml (17 fl oz/2 cups) buttermilk

750 g (1 lb 11 oz/3 cups) kewpie mayonnaise

90 ml (3 fl oz) oyster sauce

4 tbsp horseradish (fresh grated or cream), or to taste

2 cups dill fronds, finely chopped

2 cups flat-leaf (Italian) parsley, finely chopped

Add all the ingredients to a bowl and, using a fork, stir until incorporated. Taste and season with salt, freshly ground black pepper and more horseradish if you like.

To make a vegetarian version of the ranch, replace the oyster sauce with equal parts nutritional yeast flakes and hoisin. Keeps for up to 2 weeks in the fridge in a tightly sealed jar.

Cavolo nero, chorizo, preserved lemon with smoked almonds and ranch

This is the loveliest throw-together salad that hits in all the right places. Hearty green leaves, pops of lemon, a hit of spice and the creamy, herbaceous goodness of the ranch. **Serves 4**

1 tablespoon olive oil

3 chorizo sausages, skin removed, meat roughly chopped

3 garlic cloves, peeled and finely chopped

pinch of sweet smoked paprika

600 g (1 lb 5 oz) cavolo nero (Tuscan kale), leaves picked, stems discarded

½ small preserved lemon, pips discarded, skin and flesh roughly chopped

1 tablespoon lemon juice

185 ml (6 fl oz/¾ cup) Ultimate ranch dressing (page 201), or sufficient to dress the salad, not coat it

115 g (4 oz) smoked almonds, roughly chopped

1–2 avocados, stone removed, sliced

Add the oil to a frying pan over medium heat. Once hot, add the chorizo and fry for 3–5 minutes or until golden and charred in spots and some of the red-hued oil has released from the sausage. Add the garlic and cook until just starting to brown. Add the paprika, stirring to coat, then remove the chorizo and garlic from the pan.

Add the cavolo nero to the pan, in a few batches to give each a moment to cook before all has been added. Add 60 ml (¼ cup) water and season very generously with salt and freshly ground black pepper – the leaves should just be beginning to wilt down. Stir-fry for 1–2 minutes until the liquid has evaporated but the leaves still retain some bite.

Return the chorizo and garlic to the pan with the preserved lemon and lemon juice. Stir to combine, then turn into a large bowl and add the ranch dressing and almonds, folding through to combine. Add the avocado and toss again very gently to combine.

Divide among bowls or add to a large serving platter. Season again with salt and pepper and serve.

Vego hack

- Skip the chorizo for a vegetarian version and follow the substitutes for Ultimate ranch dressing on page 201

Bloody Mary and parmesan tornado ta tas

You could make these as tornados or, heck, if you can't be bothered with the skewered potato action, just add the spice blend to your Sunday night roast potatoes and serve with a dollop of the ranch; happy, happy days. Don't forget to turn your potatoes. **Serves 6**

You will need 6 metal skewers for this recipe

6 potatoes (desiree or other medium-starch potato)

2 tablespoons olive oil

45 g (1½ oz) unsalted butter, melted

50 g (1¾ oz) grated parmesan, plus extra for serving

pinch of sea salt to taste

Bloody Mary potato seasoning

1 tablespoon each celery seeds, paprika, freeze-dried tomato powder, garlic powder

generous pinch of aleppo pepper flakes

generous pinch of sea salt, plus extra to serve

Whipped ranch

250 ml (8½ fl oz/1 cup) Ultimate ranch dressing (page 201)

120 g (4½ oz) crumbled Persian feta

Preheat the oven to 180°C (360°F).

Combine the bloody Mary potato seasoning ingredients in a bowl.

Skewer the potatoes lengthways through the centre with the skewers.

To spiralise the potato, using a sharp knife, make a small cut at one end of the potato until you hit the skewer, then carefully twist the potato round to continue the cut all the way along – you will need to angle the knife slightly as you cut, moving up the potato. Don't worry about being perfect here, the aim is to create relatively uniform widths as you cut into the potato for even cooking. Once roasted, this will help create the spiralised effect.

Gently pull out the spirals to ensure even gaps along the length of the skewer, and brush well with the olive oil and butter. Repeat with the remaining potatoes.

Add the parmesan to a bowl, then add the bloody Mary potato seasoning and a good pinch of sea salt and black pepper. Sprinkle three-quarters of the mixture over the potato spirals, then line up the skewers on a baking tray. Bake for 50–65 minutes, or until cooked through and crispy. To prevent the spices from burning, turn regularly during cooking.

For the whipped ranch, add the ultimate ranch dressing and feta to a blender and give it a quick whizz – it should become gloriously creamy. Turn out into a bowl.

Remove the potatoes and sprinkle with remaining spice and parmesan mixture. Season and serve with the whipped ranch.

Broccolini, freekeh and mint salad with ranch and pistachios

Just crunchy, chewy, moreish goodness. This salad sits well for extended periods and leftovers make for a very respectable lunch the next day. And it's green, so it feels (and actually is) pretty virtuous. **Serves 4 as part of a spread**

625 ml (21 fl oz/2½ cups) vegetable or chicken stock

240 g (8½ oz) freekeh

2 bunches broccolini, thinly sliced

1 cup mint leaves, chopped

185 ml (6 fl oz/¾ cup) Ultimate ranch dressing (page 201)

35 g (1¼ oz/¼ cup) chopped pistachio kernels

Bring the stock to the boil in a saucepan over medium–high heat. Add the freekeh, reduce the heat and simmer for 30–40 minutes, or until the grains have softened and cooked through – they will still retain some bite. Strain and allow to cool.

Add the cooked freekeh to a large bowl with the sliced broccolini and mint. Season generously with salt and freshly ground black pepper. Pour most of the ranch dressing over the freekeh, reserving a few tablespoons to drizzle when serving. Sprinkle with the chopped pistachios and any extra dressing and season again with salt and pepper.

Bulk it out

- Add spinach, cavolo nero (Tuscan kale), cooked French puy lentils
- Plays well with grilled proteins. Think usual suspects: grilled salmon, chicken, lamb

Sunday slow-roasted pastrami brisket with ranch, pickles and kettles

This is perfect eating. The brisket, the ranch, the pickles, the kettle chips. The glorious hands-dirty eating of it all. It requires the kind of 'get-in-my-mouth' shovelling that you might think leads to self-consciousness, though trust me, the flavour will win over social awkwardness with this one every time. **Serves 6–8**

1 × 1.5 kg (3 lb 5 oz) brisket

1 tablespoon vegetable oil

Pastrami spice rub

2 tablespoons black peppercorns

2 tablespoons white peppercorns

2 tablespoons mustard seeds

2 tablespoons coriander seeds

1 tablespoon sea salt

½ tablespoon ground coffee

3 tablespoons smoked paprika

1 teaspoon cayenne pepper

2 tablespoons brown sugar

250 ml (8½ fl oz/1 cup) Ultimate ranch dressing (page 201)

120 g (4½ oz) sweet and spicy pickles

¼ cup flat-leaf (Italian) parsley, finely chopped

Kettle or other thick-cut chips (crisps)

For the pastrami spice rub, crush the whole spices and sea salt with a mortar and pestle, then combine with the coffee, paprika, cayenne pepper and sugar.

Sprinkle the spice rub over the brisket, making sure it is very well coated, massaging it into the meat. Refrigerate the brisket overnight, or for at least 3–4 hours, to allow the spices to flavour the meat.

Preheat the oven to 150°C (300°F).

When ready to cook, add the oil and 40 ml (1¼ fl oz) of water into a roasting dish and move it around to coat the base of the dish. Carefully transfer the brisket into the dish, cover very tightly with foil, then cook for 5 hours. Once cooked, the brisket will be soft to the touch and feel like you could just put your finger through it. Rest for 15 minutes before slicing.

Serve all the elements at the table so people can help themselves. Alternatively, you could smear the base of a plate with the ranch and add slices of brisket. You could top with some pickles and just serve the potato chips on the side.

Other options

- Serve it with Barbecue sauce (page 114) and the Barbecue sauce sweet potato salad (page 116)
- Serve it with Zhug (page 101) in a taco, sandwich or pita bread

Crisp chicken, radish pea salad and ranch

Hot, crisp chicken, cold, crunchy vegetables, and a coat of ranch. It's such a crowd pleaser and simple to throw together. It's basically a colonel burger from the 'dirty bird', but with salad. A dish for grown-ups – though small people tend to love this one just as much. **Serves 6–8**

6 skinless, boneless chicken thighs

75 g (2¾ oz/½ cup) plain (all-purpose) flour

2 organic free-range eggs, lightly whisked

120 g (4½ oz/2 cups) coarse panko breadcrumbs (I always like to have more on hand just in case)

60 ml (2 fl oz/¼ cup) rice bran oil (or other flavourless oil)

½ continental (long) cucumber, shaved into ribbons with a peeler

6 radishes, scrubbed and thinly sliced

65 g (2¼ oz/½ cup) frozen peas, blanched in boiling water

50 g (½ cup) sugar snap peas, trimmed and cut lengthways

185 ml (6 fl oz/¾ cup) Ultimate ranch dressing (page 201), plus extra to serve on the side

Preheat the oven to 180°C (360°F).

Set three shallow bowls along your kitchen bench and add, from left to right, the flour, followed by the whisked egg, and finally the panko.

Roll the thighs out so they are flat (no need to flatten them with a mallet), then coat each fillet in the flour before dredging in the egg and finally coating in the panko crumbs. Season with salt and freshly ground black pepper.

Place an ovenproof frying pan over medium–high heat. Add the oil and, once shimmering, add the chicken, being careful not to overcrowd the pan. Cook for 1–3 minutes or until the chicken takes on a lovely golden colour. Flip the chicken, then pop the pan in the oven for 6 minutes or until the chicken has cooked through.

Remove the chicken from the oven and cut into thick slices.

Layer the cucumber, radishes, peas and sugar snaps on a plate and top with the sliced chicken. Drizzle with the ranch and season with salt and pepper. Serve with additional ranch on the side.

Serve hot, to best enjoy the crisp hot chicken against the cooling fresh vegetables.

Ultimate ranch dressing

Jalapeño jam

Liquorice jam

Quince jam

Well, I'll be jammed

No longer reserved for old-fashioned high teas and cheese platters, a good jam – one with sweet and/or savoury leanings – is an exercise in riotous colour and wake-me-up flavours. A little dabble here or a smear there can levitate the simplest of foods. It can be the star of a dish, the back-up singer marinade, or the whole band if you so desire. At the very least, you'll use one of those old jars in the back of the cupboard and be guaranteed you'll get the lid off. Nothing is more frustrating than handing over the unopened jar of jam for lid removal and enduring the subsequent displays of strength and/or masculinity when all you want is the damn jam. Here are a few of my favourites.

Jalapeño jam

The perfect launch pad for all your food-wolfing shenanigans.
I'm pretty sure this will last in a sterilised jar as long as you and I would.

To make 945 g
(2 lb 1 oz/3 cups)

1 tbsp olive oil

2 green capsicums (bell peppers), deseeded and diced

2 red onions, peeled and roughly chopped

5 fresh jalapeños, sliced (deseed if you prefer a milder relish)

230 g (8 oz/1 cup) caster sugar

250 ml (8½ fl oz/1 cup) apple cider vinegar

salt and freshly ground black pepper

1 cup coriander (cilantro) leaves, washed and thinly sliced

To make 1.25 kg
(2 lb 12 oz/4 cups)

1½ tbsp olive oil

3 green capsicums (bell peppers), deseeded and diced

3 red onions, peeled and roughly chopped

7 fresh jalapeños, sliced (deseed if you prefer a milder relish)

345 g (12 oz/1½ cups) caster sugar

375 ml (12½ fl oz/1½ cups) apple cider vinegar

salt and freshly ground black pepper

1½ cups coriander (cilantro) leaves, washed and thinly sliced

To make 1.9 kg
(4 lb 7 oz/6 cups)

2 tbsp olive oil

4 green capsicums (bell peppers), deseeded and diced

4 red onions, peeled and roughly chopped

10 fresh jalapeños, sliced (deseed if you prefer a milder relish)

460 g (1 lb/2 cups) caster sugar

500 ml (17 fl oz/2 cups) apple cider vinegar

salt and freshly ground black pepper

2 cups coriander (cilantro) leaves, washed and thinly sliced

Add the olive oil to a large saucepan over medium–low heat. Once the oil is warm, add the capsicum, onion and jalapeño and cook, stirring often, for 20 minutes or until soft. Add the sugar and apple cider vinegar and cook for a further 20 minutes or until the liquid has reduced to a jammy, syrup-like consistency. Add salt and freshly ground black pepper to taste.

Remove from the heat and allow to cool before adding to a blender with the coriander leaves and pulsing briefly until a relish consistency, then spoon into sterilised jars.

A few other things you might like to do with it

- Add to a cheese platter – let quince paste have a rest. Goes superbly with soft goat's cheese and the like.
- Add to a bucket of aïoli for pure, unadulterated hot chip, crudité, chicken-wing-dipping pleasure.
- Glaze it on alllll the proteins before roasting.
- Smear on toast with your breakfast eggs.

Tuna, jalapeño and yuzu

If there was one dish that could sustain me an entire summer, it is this. Exactly what I want and love to eat. Bright, fresh, oven-free and a dish that takes literally seconds to throw together. With a scoop 'n' dip scenario, cutlery is optional. **Serves 6 as a snack**

160 g (5½ oz/½ cup) Jalapeño jam (page 215), plus extra to serve

300 g (10½ oz) sashimi-grade tuna, cut into small cubes

2 tablespoons yuzu juice (substitute lime juice if unavailable)

2 teaspoons yuzu kosho (if unavailable, finely dice a jalapeño to substitute)

coriander (cilantro) leaves and organic unsprayed edible flowers, to scatter

90 g (3 oz) corn chips

Add the jalapeño jam to the centre of a serving plate and smear it out in a rough circle. Top with the tuna. Drizzle the yuzu juice over and dot with the yuzu kosho or minced jalapeño. Scatter with coriander leaves and edible flowers and season generously with salt and freshly ground black pepper.

Serve with corn chips, extra jalapeño jam and icy-cold beers for pure gustatory pleasure.

Jalapeño jam

Late summer nights grilled watermelon with jalapeño jam salsa

This is the 'too hot, can't handle the heat' dish of our dreams. I know grilling watermelon is a journey too far for some. Like a roller-coaster, some people are completely thrilled, while others hop off muttering 'never again'. But it imparts a brilliant smoky flavour and mellows the bright sweetness. Bucketloads of lime juice with the Jalapeño jam turn this into the condiment/sauce/dressing situation of your summer dreams. **Serves 4–6**

6 slices seedless watermelon

2 tablespoons olive oil

1 avocado, stoned and cut into small cubes

1 small Lebanese (short) cucumber, trimmed and cut into small cubes

½ cup coriander (cilantro) leaves, finely chopped, plus a few leaves to scatter

160 g (5½ oz/½ cup) Jalapeño jam (page 215), plus extra to serve

juice of 2 limes

1 jalapeño, sliced

Heat a barbecue grill plate to high. Toss the slices of watermelon in the olive oil to coat then grill for 2 minutes per side, turning once.

While the watermelon is grilling, combine the avocado, cucumber, coriander and jalapeño jam in a bowl with a drizzle of lime juice and gently use a fork to combine. Season with salt and freshly ground black pepper.

Place the grilled watermelon onto a serving plate and immediately squeeze over the juice of 1 lime while the watermelon is still hot. Top with the salsa and more lime juice and scatter over the extra coriander leaves and sliced jalapeño. Serve some extra jalapeño jam on the side.

Cheese sticks for adults

Crispy cheese sticks. For adults. Pretty sure it doesn't get much better than that. No back chatting. That's how we roll. **Serves 4**

300 g (10½ oz) crumbled
    Persian feta

4 tablespoons finely chopped
    coriander (cilantro)

zest of 1 unwaxed lime

1 teaspoon ground chipotle

125 g (4½ oz) Jalapeño jam
    (page 215) plus extra 60 g (2 oz)
    to serve

16–20 sheets filo pastry

45 g (1½ oz) unsalted butter, melted

Preheat the oven to 180°C (360°F). Line a large baking tray with baking paper.

Combine the feta, coriander, lime zest, chipotle and jalapeño jam in a bowl. Using a fork, mash and incorporate the elements until you have a soft and pliable mixture.

Place 2–3 sheets of filo on a flat work surface and cut in half lengthways, then cut each half into two triangles. Place 1½ tablespoons (approximately) on the long end of the dough. Roll the filo up over the filling, folding the side edges in to ensure none of the filling escapes while cooking. Place on the prepared baking tray and repeat to make between 14 and 16 rolls.

Generously brush the rolls with the melted butter, then pop in the oven and cook for 18–20 minutes or until the rolls look crisp and golden.

To serve, smear the base of a serving plate with jalapeño jam. Top with the rolls and serve hot – with a warning so people don't burn the roof of their mouths as they attempt to inhale them!

This is a hands in, grab, smear, eat situation. I suggest subtly putting a few hand towels within reach.

Jalapeño jam

Mescal-marinated steak salad with charred pineapple, jalapeño jam and herbs

Take me to Mexico. Or make me this salad. Two simple requests really. Also, one far more likely than the other. **Serves 4**

3–4 sirloin or minute steaks

4 tablespoons olive oil

2 garlic cloves, grated

½ tablespoon coriander seeds, roughly ground

60 ml (2 fl oz/¼ cup) mezcal

8 slices of fresh pineapple

250 g (9 oz) sweet cherry tomatoes, quartered

125 g (4½ oz) Jalapeño jam (page 215), plus extra to serve

juice of 1 lime

1 avocado, stoned and cubed

1 large bunch of coriander (cilantro), rinsed and leaves roughly chopped

Place the steaks, half the olive oil, the garlic, ground coriander and mezcal in a bowl. Toss to coat and set aside for an hour at room temperature to marinate.

Heat a large non-stick frying pan over high heat. Add the pineapple slices and cook for 1–2 minutes each side or until starting to char and take on colour. Remove and allow to cool before cutting into cubes. Depending on how ripe your pineapple is, you may like to discard the core. If the fruit is ripe and has had a little time in the frying pan, it is often fine to eat. Add to a bowl with the cherry tomatoes, jalapeño jam, lime juice, avocado and fresh coriander and toss very gently to combine. You want to incorporate the jalapeño jam across the elements, but you don't want to bruise the avocado or cause the pineapple to juice and make your salad a boggy mess.

Drain the beef from the marinade and return the frying pan to medium heat. Add the remaining oil and, once hot, cook, turning once, until done to your liking, 2–3 minutes each side for medium-rare. Transfer to a plate and rest for 5 minutes before slicing into thick slices.

Add the pineapple and jalapeño jam salad to bowls and top with the sliced steak. Add a little more jalapeño jam and season generously with salt and freshly ground black pepper.

This is best served while the steak is still warm but, honestly, it's the perfect cold salad on a hot day whatever temperature it comes.

Jalapeño jam

Corn and chickpea salad with miso jalapeño tahini dressing

Corn and jalapeño belong together. The heat and the sweet is always a killer combo. This salad is best made at the last minute. I use dollops of the Jalapeño jam in both the salad itself and as part of the dressing. You can make the dressing and the crispy chickpeas ahead of time, so assembly labour is minimal. **Serves 4–6 as a generous side**

3 corn cobs

2 tablespoons olive oil

sea salt flakes

60 g (2 oz) Jalapeño jam (page 215)

1 avocado, stoned and sliced

1 large bunch of coriander (cilantro), rinsed and leaves coarsely torn

1 large bunch of basil, leaves picked

Dressing

1 jalapeño, deseeded and chopped

80 g (2¾ oz) Jalapeño jam (page 215)

1 thumbnail-size piece fresh ginger, grated

2 small garlic cloves, finely grated

¼ cup coriander (cilantro) leaves

juice and zest of 1 unwaxed lime

2 tablespoons tahini

2 teaspoons white miso

3 tablespoons iced water

Crispy chickpeas

400 g (14 oz) tinned chickpeas, drained and rinsed thoroughly

2 tablespoons olive oil

1 teaspoon each ground chipotle, oregano, sweet smoked paprika and cumin

To make the dressing, purée the jalapeño, jalapeño jam, ginger, garlic, coriander, lime juice, tahini, miso and iced water in a blender until smooth. Season with salt.

Preheat the oven to 170°C (340°F). Line a baking tray with baking paper.

For the crispy chickpeas, combine the chickpeas, olive oil and spices in a bowl and toss to coat. Turn out onto the prepared tray and pop in the oven to crisp, about 15 minutes.

While the chickpeas are roasting, heat a barbecue to high or place a chargrill pan over high heat. Lightly brush the corn with the olive oil and scatter with sea salt flakes. Grill the corn, turning occasionally, until lightly charred, 15–20 minutes – you'll have some black, brown and yellow kernels. Set aside until cool enough to handle – about 2–3 minutes – then remove the kernels from the cobs, by slicing as close to the cobs as possible with a sharp knife.

Add the corn and chickpeas to a large serving platter. Dollop the jalapeño jam on top and drizzle with the dressing. Top with the avocado and herbs and season generously with salt and freshly ground black pepper.

Want a few suggestions to try it with?

- Wine. Always.
- After that, try it with Barbecued roasted chicken with spiced whipped feta (page 118)

Jalapeño-jam-addled fish burritos

Never met a fish taco I didn't like. The trend continues. **Serves 4**

Marinated fish

50 g (1¾ oz) coriander (cilantro) leaves and young stems

2 teaspoons ground paprika

1 teaspoon ground cumin

6 tablespoons Jalapeño jam (page 215)

zest of 1 unwaxed lime

80 ml (2½ fl oz/⅓ cup) olive oil

750 g (1 lb 11 oz) snapper or blue-eye cod fillets (any firm white fish works well)

Salad

1 telegraph (long) cucumber shaved into ribbons

250 g (9 oz) cherry tomatoes, sliced in half

4 spring onions (scallions), sliced

handful of coriander (cilantro) leaves

juice of ½ lime

1 avocado, peeled and stoned

2 jalapeños, thinly sliced

To serve

tortillas

¾ cup kewpie mayonnaise

juice of 1 lime

Jalapeño jam

For the marinated fish, add all the ingredients, except for the fish, to a blender and give it a brief blitz to get a paste.

Place the fish in a large bowl, add the paste and turn gently to coat. Pop in the fridge to marinate for 20 minutes. Bring to room temperature when you are ready to cook.

Add all the salad items to a large serve-yourself platter.

Heat a non-stick frying pan over high heat. When hot, add some of the fish in a single layer and cook for 2 minutes. Turn and cook on the other side for 1 minute or until the fish is opaque and just cooked – the sugar in the jalapeño jam should give it some glorious caramelised edges.

While the fish is cooking, wrap the tortillas in foil and pop them in a 200°C (390°F) oven for 5 minutes to warm through – or give them a sojourn through the microwave on high for 30–45 seconds.

To make a lime mayonnaise combine the kewpie mayonnaise and lime juice in a bowl.

To serve, place the fish, the plate of salad items, the lime mayonnaise and the extra jalapeño jam on a table for the spoon-adding, ingredient-scooping, lettuce-escaping burrito-building pleasure.

Liquorice jam

I understand people love or hate liquorice. There is no middle ground, and I am okay with its glorious, polarising qualities. I like to think it's my Dutch heritage, and I was born with a taste for it in my blood. I love that it can range from sweet to bitter, there is an intensity to it, and the hit of molasses and aniseed is pure hedonistic pleasure. Here it is broken down into a jam-like consistency – one you can scoop from the fridge with a spoon or add to your cooking at a moment's notice. Dark corn syrup can be found at specialist grocers. You can, in a liquorice-requiring emergency, substitute the syrup with dark brown sugar, but be aware it will have a slightly grainier finish. Also, I'm not one normally to colour food, but this benefits hugely from some black food colouring gel – you'll thank me later.

To make 400 g
(14 oz/1 cup)

25 g (1 oz) unsalted butter

115 g (4 oz/½ cup) caster (superfine) sugar

60 ml (2 fl oz/¼ cup) dark corn syrup (or dark agave syrup)

60 ml (2 fl oz/¼ cup) sweetened condensed milk

2 tbsp molasses (use blackstrap for the strongest flavour)

pinch of kosher salt

½ tsp black food colouring gel

2 tsp anise seeds, finely ground

To make 800 g
(1 lb 12 oz/2 cups)

50 g (1¾ oz) unsalted butter

230 g (8 oz/1 cup) caster (superfine) sugar

120 ml (4 fl oz/¼ cup) dark corn syrup (or dark agave syrup)

120 ml (4 fl oz/½ cup) sweetened condensed milk

80 ml (2½ fl oz) molasses (use blackstrap for the strongest flavour)

pinch of kosher salt

1 tsp black food colouring gel

3 tsp anise seeds, finely ground

To make 1.2 kg
(2 lb 10 oz/3 cups)

75g unsalted butter

460 g (1 lb/2 cups) caster (superfine) sugar

180 ml (6 fl oz/¼ cup) dark corn syrup (or dark agave syrup)

180 ml (6 fl oz/¾ cup) sweetened condensed milk

100 ml (3½ fl oz) molasses (use blackstrap for the strongest flavour)

pinch of kosher salt

1½ tsp black food colouring gel

5 tsp anise seeds, finely ground

Add the butter, sugar, dark corn syrup, sweetened condensed milk, molasses and salt to a saucepan over medium heat and bring to a gentle boil. Stir the mixture frequently to prevent scorching in the corners or sticking to the bottom. Attach a sugar thermometer. Once the mixture reaches 105°C (220°F), remove it from the heat and immediately stir in the ground aniseed and black food gel. Once they're fully incorporated, pour the mixture into a sterilised jar. It will firm further as it cools. This will keep in a screw-top jar in a cool spot in your pantry for 3–4 months.

If you fancy making your own liquorice ...

Make the jam in the 2 cup quantity above and, as you stir in the aniseed, add 60 g (2 oz) sifted plain (all-purpose) flour and whisk like the clappers until fully incorporated. This is an arm workout like no other – one worthy of a fitspo social media account. Turn out the mixture and roll using your hands into a liquorice strap-like shape. Cut into pieces, allow to cool and store in an airtight container. This will keep up to 2 weeks.

Well, I'll be jammed

230

Chocolate liquorice thumbprints

Dense, with plenty of chew, and the most intriguing smoky undertone thanks to the liquorice. This would rival any Country Women's Association jam drop any day. **Makes 23 x 30 g (1 oz) balls**

240 g (8½ oz) plain (all-purpose) flour

85 g (3 oz) Dutch (unsweetened) cocoa powder

230 g (8 oz) unsalted butter, at room temperature

200 g (7 oz) caster (superfine) sugar

2 teaspoons vanilla bean extract

2 large organic free-range egg yolks

55 g (2 oz/¼ cup) granulated sugar, for rolling

300 g (10½ oz/¾ cup) Liquorice jam (page 228)

Ganache

200 g (7 oz) couverture dark chocolate, chopped (at least 70%)

150 ml (5 fl oz) pouring (single/light) cream

To serve

freeze-dried fruits and edible dried flowers, to scatter

Preheat the oven to 180°C (360°F). Line two large baking trays with baking paper.

Whisk together the flour, cocoa and a pinch of salt in a bowl.

In the bowl of a stand mixer fitted with the paddle attachment, beat the butter and caster sugar until pale and creamy, about 5 minutes. Add the vanilla to incorporate. Scrape down the side of the bowl, then add the yolks, one at a time, until fully incorporated. Turn the speed to low and add the flour mixture. Beat until a soft dough has begun to form – this will be very quick, and you don't want to overwork the dough here.

Tip the granulated sugar into a separate bowl. Roll a tablespoon of the mixture at a time into a smooth ball, then roll in the sugar and place on the prepared trays. Repeat with the remaining dough. Ensure the balls are placed apart as they will spread when cooking. With your thumb, make a small well-like indent in the middle of each, not pushing so far down that you touch the bottom.

Bake for 10–12 minutes, rotating the baking trays halfway through. The indents will have puffed, so gently push down on them. If they are too hot, use the end of a wooden spoon or salad server. Allow to cool completely.

To make the ganache, warm the cream in a separate saucepan over medium–low heat, then add the dark chocolate, whisking constantly until fully incorporated.

Spoon about a teaspoon of liquorice jam into each cookie. Drizzle with chocolate ganache, just to cover. Leave to stand for a few minutes so the ganache thickens. Adorn with freeze-dried fruits, crystallised violets or edible flowers.

Best eaten on the day of making but can keep in a container for a few days.

Caramelised white chocolate ganache, liquorice and raspberry tarts

White chocolate. Liquorice. Raspberry. Quite possibly the combination that birthed the term *ménage à trois*. **Makes 6 tarts**

butter, for greasing

1 × 320 g (11½ oz) sheet sweet vanilla bean pastry

400 g (14 oz/1 cup) Liquorice jam (page 228), warmed to a malleable temperature

250 g (9 oz) raspberries

1½ tablespoons vanilla bean paste

Ganache

200 g (7 oz) couverture white chocolate, chopped (at least 30% cocoa butter)

150 ml (5 fl oz) pouring (single/ light) cream

Preheat the oven to 180°C (360°F).

Grease six 9 cm (3½ in) fluted non-stick flan (tart) tins with butter, carefully pushing it up the sides into the flutes. Trim the overhang, then let the tarts sit in the fridge for 20 minutes.

Line the tart shells with baking paper, then fill with pastry weights or rice. Blind bake for 15 minutes, then carefully remove the weights and the baking paper and return to the oven and continue to cook until golden and the pastry is uniform in colour, about 10 minutes, noting the centre base of the tart, this will be the last section to cook.

Add the liquorice jam to a small saucepan over very low heat. Stir regularly until it is a malleable, spreadable consistency.

Add the raspberries and 1 tablespoon vanilla bean paste to a bowl and use a fork to break up the raspberries a little to release their juice.

Add about 1½ tablespoons of the warmed liquorice jam to the base of each tart and, using a small spoon, gently spread the jam across the base. Cover with about 1 tablespoon macerated raspberries.

For caramelised white chocolate, stir the chocolate continuously in a small saucepan over low heat until melted, golden and caramelised, 20–25 minutes. This is rather laborious and I have been known to swap out with good ole Caramilk when time isn't on my side. No judgement here. Chocolate is chocolate, let's all remember where we came from.

Warm the cream in a separate saucepan over medium–low heat, then add the caramelised chocolate, whisking constantly until fully incorporated. Add the remaining vanilla bean paste and a very good pinch of salt. Whisk again, then gently pour the mixture over the tarts. Pop in the fridge for 2–3 hours or until set.

Best enjoyed the day of making.

Hava Heart chocolate caramel ice cream

Hava Heart, the classic Australian heart-shaped, chocolate-covered ice cream on a stick, has a special place in my heart. Before Magnums entered stage left, this was my father's ice cream of choice. I don't recall a childhood holiday without seeing him go for one of these and it is one of my dearest memories of summer and the beach. You will need heart-shaped chocolate ice block (popsicle) moulds for this recipe. The benefit is, you can make these in stages over a few days, keeping your kitchen toils to a workable minimum. **Makes 6–8**

1 litre (34 fl oz/4 cups) excellent-quality vanilla bean ice cream, softened

125 g (4½ oz) Liquorice jam (page 228), warmed to malleable consistency, or to taste

500 g (1 lb 2 oz) dark couverture chocolate (60% cocoa solids), finely chopped and melted (or if you prefer a lighter touch, replace with excellent-quality couverture milk chocolate – chocolate is personal; I get it.)

90 ml (3 fl oz) dulche de leche

Add the ice cream and liquorice jam to a bowl and, using a whisk, stir to fully incorporate the jam through the ice cream. It will get quite soft during this process and if you make this in the height of summer, simply pop the bowl into the freezer for little 5-minute power naps so you don't end up with a liquified ice cream. You want to keep it at a malleable, but still relatively firm, consistency. Taste and check you get a strong but not overpowering liquorice flavour. Adjust as necessary and to your taste.

Melt 150 g (5½ oz) of the chocolate in a heatproof bowl placed over a saucepan of simmering water, making sure water doesn't touch bowl. Add about 1 tablespoon of chocolate per heart mould, then pop in the freezer to quickly set, about 15 minutes. Once set, add ½ tablespoon dulche de leche on top of the chocolate. Scoop the liquorice ice cream mixture into the mould and smooth until flat, using the back of a spoon. Gently tap the mould on the kitchen bench to release any air bubbles, then place in the freezer to set, at least 4 hours.

Melt the remaining chocolate in a heatproof bowl by placing the bowl over a saucepan of simmering water, ensuring the water isn't touching the sides of the bowl. As soon as it has melted remove the pan from the heat, cool slightly, then working quickly with one ice cream heart at a time, coat the hearts in chocolate and return them to the freezer (if the chocolate becomes too thick, gently melt it again). Freeze the liquorice hava-hearts until very firm (4–5 hours), then serve.

Slow-cooked liquorice short ribs

Beef short ribs, cooked slowly until practically slipping off the bone, are one of life's greatest pleasures. This one is for the weekend, when slow-cooking is the order of the day and you have the time and inclination to fill your house with the wondrous smell of dinner, long before it is needed. **Serves 4–6**

2 tablespoons olive oil

2 kg (4 lb 6 oz) beef short ribs

2 French shallots, peeled and sliced

3 garlic cloves

½ tablespoon coriander seeds, toasted in a dry pan until fragrant, then roughly ground

300 g (10½ oz/¾ cup) Liquorice jam (page 228)

1 knob fresh ginger, grated

2 cinnamon sticks

375 ml (12½ fl oz/1½ cups) ginger beer

1 litre (34 fl oz/4 cups) beef bone broth

1 tablespoon Chinese black vinegar

steamed rice, to serve

limes, to serve

Asian salad

1 telegraph (long) cucumber, julienned (or shave into ribbons using a peeler)

1 large red chilli, deseeded and very finely julienned

1 cup coriander (cilantro) leaves, thinly sliced

80 g (2¾ oz/½ cup) salted peanuts, roughly chopped

fried shallots

Preheat the oven to 180°C (360°F).

Heat the oil in a wide, heavy-based ovenproof saucepan over high heat. Once hot, add the ribs and brown them all over, 3–5 minutes. Remove from the pan and transfer the ribs to a bowl. Add the shallots, garlic and coriander seeds to the pan, lower the heat and cook until fragrant and soft but not yet browning, about 5 minutes. Add the liquorice jam, grated ginger and cinnamon sticks and stir constantly until the liquorice jam looks as if it's dissolving and coating the mixture. Return the ribs to the pan. Cover with the ginger beer, broth and Chinese black vinegar.

Cover the pan, transfer to the oven and braise until the meat falls from the bone, about 4–4½ hours. I recommend checking this about halfway through the cooking time to ensure the liquid isn't reducing too rapidly – given the variability in oven heat, it can often be reducing rapidly or not fast enough. If it looks like there is insufficient liquid, add more beef bone broth, about 250 ml (1 cup) at a time and continue cooking. You don't want the ribs to be drowning but there needs to be enough liquid to ensure they aren't sticking to the base of the pot, drying out and burning.

While the beef is cooking, add the salad items to a bowl and use your hands to toss gently to combine.

Once the beef ribs are cooked, gently remove the rib bones from the liquid and set aside.

Check that the braising liquid has reduced – you want it to have reduced by about half. If not, place over medium heat until reduced. Using a couple of forks, shred the meat in the sauce – it should be glossy and gelatinous and smell completely fragrant and amazing. Season with salt and freshly ground black pepper.

Add the rice to serving bowls, top with the liquorice beef and some salad. Squeeze over the lime juice and serve.

Brown sugar pav with liquorice jam and passionfruit

You'd probably be appalled, but the story goes: one day I was contemplating a piece of liquorice in front of a brown sugar meringue and they both fell into my mouth at the same time. Who knew liquorice and meringue and passionfruit belonged together? Anyone who makes this recipe. The acidity of the passionfruit, the sweetness of the meringue and the unifying flavour of the liquorice give a perfect bite. **Serves 8–10**

Brown sugar pavlova

6 organic free-range egg whites

200 g (7 oz) caster (superfine) sugar

165 g (6 oz/¾ cup, firmly packed) brown sugar

1 tablespoon vanilla bean paste

1 tablespoon apple cider vinegar

To top

250 ml (8½ fl oz/1 cup) thickened (whipping) cream

1 tablespoon vanilla bean paste

chunks of white chocolate (optional but highly recommended)

125 g (4½ oz) Liquorice jam (page 228), warmed in a saucepan

pulp from 4 passionfruit

organic unsprayed edible flowers, to scatter (optional)

Preheat the oven to 130°C (265°F). Grease a large flat baking tray and line it with baking paper.

For the pavlova, beat the egg whites in a large, clean bowl using an electric whisk or in a stand mixer fitted with the whisk attachment, until soft peaks form. Gradually beat in the sugars, 1 tablespoon at a time, until the meringue is thick and glossy. Whisk in the vanilla bean paste and the vinegar until incorporated.

Spoon the meringue mixture into the middle of the prepared baking tray and spread out into a roughly 20–25 cm (10 in) circle. Bake for 1½–1¾ hours – you want it to look crisp but not coloured. Turn off the oven and leave the pavlova to cool completely inside.

When ready to serve, whisk the cream to medium peaks, then add the vanilla bean paste and whisk just to combine. Stir through the chocolate chunks. Dollop the mixture over the top of the pavlova. Drizzle over the warmed liquorice jam, then top with the passionfruit pulp and edible flowers. Best eaten immediately.

Quince jam

I love how this gnarly, ugly fruit, once harnessed, soothed, treated and rustled, comes perfectly alive. Paired with spices, zests and florals it becomes something entirely new – it is robust and glorious in colour, taste and texture. It can run the gamut from savoury through sweet with ease. Quince jam is something that should always be home-made. The kinds bought in stores are often overly sweet, sometimes artificial in taste, or scant on quince and heavy on the fillers. And they cost a fortune, which is confusing given all it needs is a few fruits and some time on the stove for a fraction of the price. Make your own.

To make 945 g
(2 lb 1 oz/3 cups)

2 quinces (approx. 600 g/ 1 lb 5 oz) peeled, cored and quartered

230 g (8 oz/1 cup) caster (superfine) sugar

1 vanilla bean, halved, seeds scraped

2 cardamom pods, bruised

juice of 1 lemon

500 ml (17 fl oz/2 cups) water

To make 1.9 kg
(4 lb 7 oz/6 cups)

4 quinces, (approx. 1.2 kg/ 2 lb 10 oz) peeled, cored and quartered

460 g (1 lb/2 cups) caster (superfine) sugar

1 vanilla bean, halved, seeds scraped

4 cardamom pods, bruised

juice of 1 lemon

1 litre (34 fl oz/4 cups) water

To make 2.8 kg
(6 lb/9 cups)

6 quinces (approx. 1.8 kg/ 4 lb) peeled, cored and quartered

690 g (1½ lb/3 cups) caster (superfine) sugar

1–2 vanilla beans, halved, seeds scraped

6 cardamom pods, bruised

juice of 1 lemon

1.5 litres (51 fl oz/6 cups) water

Add all the ingredients to a large saucepan and give them a few swirls with a wooden spoon to incorporate. Cover with a lid and cook until the quinces are soft and have taken on a glorious pinky red sunset hue. This can take 2–3 hours, sometimes more. You want the residual liquid to look thick and syrupy. If this hasn't happened but the fruit seems ready, crank the heat and reduce it, stirring constantly to prevent any burning. Given the sugar content, it's important to keep an eye on things so you don't have a burned mess sticking to the base of your pan if your heat has been a little on the high side.

Strain to capture the vanilla and cardamom pods, then return the fruit to the liquid. Using a fork, squish and roughly pulp the fruit into the liquid until you have a chunky jam consistency. Pour into sterilised jars until ready to use.

You can also throw all of this in the slow-cooker on low for 8 hours, then follow the directions from straining the fruit onwards for the same result. You will just need to reduce the liquid on the stovetop first as little to no evaporation will have occurred and you will have more liquid than if you prepared this on the stove. This will keep for up to 6 months in a screw-top jar in the fridge.

The multitasker – quince roast chicken with saffron, olives and potatoes

This could work for dinner on the least busy day of the week, as much as it could be plonked on the table when friends are around. Sear the chicken skin, then shove the lot in the oven to do its thing. A quick stovetop reduction and you've got everything you need in life – crisp, soft, salty, sweet, and carb. In other words, the perfect meal. **Serves 4**

50 g (1¾ oz) unsalted butter, softened

2 garlic cloves, crushed

160 g (5½ oz) Quince jam (page 238)

1 organic free-range chicken, halved

5 floury potatoes, such as kestrel

1 tablespoon olive oil

150 g (5½ oz) pitted Sicilian green olives

250 ml (8½ fl oz/1 cup) white wine

250 ml (8½ fl oz/1 cup) chicken stock

pinch of saffron threads

5–10 cavolo nero (Tuscan kale) leaves

Preheat the oven to 170°C (340°F).

Add the butter, garlic and quince jam to a bowl and use a fork to combine.

Gently loosen the skin of the chicken with your fingers and push in the butter mixture. This bit is messy, but it's not dinner if you don't get involved with your meal. Try to spread the mixture as evenly as possible.

Bring a large saucepan of water to the boil over high heat. Add the potatoes and cook for 10 minutes until par-boiled, then drain and set aside. Once cool, cut into quarters.

Place a large ovenproof frying pan over medium heat. Add 1 tablespoon of olive oil and gently add the chicken, skin side down. Cook down the skin while the potatoes are cooking.

At the 10-minute mark, gently turn the chicken. Add the remaining ingredients, except for the cavolo nero, along with the potatoes and place in the oven to cook, uncovered, for 1 hour.

Remove from the oven and return to the stovetop over medium heat. Add the cavolo nero leaves – just nestle them in wherever you can find a spot. You want to reduce the residual liquid until it is a glorious, syrupy consistency, about 10 minutes and the kale leaves have just softened.

Season generously with salt and freshly ground black pepper and serve.

Pear and quince crumble

There's a reason crumbles continue to be such a treasured dessert. It's something that only tastes good when home-made. A restaurant crumble is something to be wary of, while the home-made version takes time, and will be richer and crunchier than you could possibly hope for. It really is the perfect dish, especially when served with ice cream or cream. By using the Quince jam here, there is no added sugar, purely harnessing the sweetness of the jam and residual fruit sugar of the pears. Adding puffed quinoa to the topping ensures a dynamic long-lasting crunch. **Serves 8**

5 pears, cored, peeled and chopped

1 teaspoon vanilla bean paste

juice and zest of ½ unwaxed lemon

315 g (11 oz/1 cup) Quince jam (page 238)

Crumble mix

100 g (3½ oz) unsalted butter

75 g (2¾ oz/2 cup) plain (all-purpose) flour

100 g (3½ oz lightly packed), soft brown sugar

45 g (1½ oz) rolled (porridge) oats

6 g (½ cup) puffed quinoa

Preheat the oven to 170°C (340°F).

For the crumble mix, add all the ingredients to a medium bowl and, using your hands, incorporate the butter until you have a coarse crumb. A few chunky streaks of butter are treasured here.

Add the pears, vanilla and lemon juice and zest to a small saucepan over medium heat. Cook for about 10–15 minutes, stirring regularly to prevent the fruit from catching – you want it to be soft, but still holding shape.

Transfer the pear mixture to a baking dish and top with dollops of the quince jam across the top. Add the crumble mixture and gently press down. Pop in the oven for 30–40 minutes or until the top is golden and you see flashes of bubbling fruit underneath.

Serve with ice cream or cream.

Mix-tape crumble

- Make a gorgonzola cream by combining a hunk of gorgonzola with some crème fraîche and take this crumble into cheese-board territory.

- Add a heft of rosewater with the fruit mixture and incorporate chunks of halva into the crumble mix for a glorious tweak.

Quince jam

Quince jam, yoghurt panna cotta with rye crumb and lemon thyme

If only life could be this pre-assembled. I love the make-ahead capacity of this panna cotta. It's the Ikea of desserts. No allen key required. You're welcome. **Serves about 6**

Panna cotta

1 kg (2 lb 3 oz) thick Greek yoghurt

1 tablespoon vanilla bean paste

2 titanium-strength gelatine leaves

600 ml (20½ fl oz) thickened (whipping) cream

75 g (2¾ oz) chopped couverture white chocolate

2 tablespoons Quince jam (page 238) per serve

Rye crumb

50 g (1¾ oz/½ cup) milk powder

40 g (¼ cup) rye flour

2 tablespoons cornflour (cornstarch)

2 tablespoons caster (superfine) sugar

60 g (2 oz) melted unsalted butter

100 g (3½ oz) couverture white chocolate, melted

25 g (1 oz) milk powder

1 tablespoon lemon thyme leaves

For the panna cotta, combine the yoghurt and vanilla bean paste in a bowl and stir until thoroughly incorporated.

Submerge the gelatine sheets in a bowl of icy cold water to bloom. They will need to feel soft and pliable; gummy-like.

Add the cream and white chocolate to a saucepan and place over low heat. Whisk constantly to prevent catching and cook until the white chocolate has melted and is fully incorporated. Remove from the heat and whisk in the bloomed gelatine thoroughly. Pour the cream mixture into the yoghurt mixture and whisk again until thoroughly combined.

Scoop the quince jam evenly among serving bowls or glasses. Top with the panna cotta mixture. Cover the bowls tightly with plastic wrap and place in the fridge overnight to set.

Preheat the oven to 170°C (340°F). Line a baking tray with baking paper.

To make the rye crumb, add the milk powder, rye flour, cornflour, sugar and a pinch of salt to a bowl. Toss to mix, then add the melted butter and toss loosely with your hands until the mixture starts to form clusters, similar to a crumble topping. Spread on the prepared baking tray, then bake in the oven for 20 minutes. The crumbs should be sandy and smell very buttery.

Add the crumbs to a bowl and add the milk powder, tossing until it seems distributed between the crumbs. Pour over the melted chocolate and toss until the clusters are covered in chocolate and the chocolate has started to harden and the clumps are no longer sticky. You can speed up this process by spreading the mixture on a tray and then popping it in the fridge.

Scatter the rye crumbs over the top of the panna cotta. Sprinkle with lemon thyme leaves and serve.

Quince and pistachio buckwheat galette

The rougher a galette is around the edges, the more beautiful it looks with its overladen fruit inappropriately oozing and bubbling. If only more baking escapades followed this formula. The buckwheat adds a brilliant nutty flavour and it's a no-brainer dessert for any crowd. **Serves 8**

Galette pastry

1½ teaspoons caster (superfine) sugar

pinch of salt

100 g (3½ oz/¾ cup) buckwheat flour

80 g (2¾ oz) plain (all-purpose) flour

65 g (2¼ oz) unsalted butter, cut into small pieces

1 organic free-range egg yolk

1 tablespoon iced water

1 teaspoon vanilla bean paste

Filling

315 g (11 oz/1 cup) Quince jam (page 238)

125 g (4½ oz) fresh raspberries

zest of ½ unwaxed lemon

To finish

1 organic free-range egg yolk

1 tablespoon pouring (single/light) cream

1 teaspoon ground cardamom

1 tablespoon sugar

raw (demerara) sugar, to scatter

pistachios, to scatter

ice cream or cream (an optional but glorious extra)

For the pastry, combine the caster sugar, salt and flours in a bowl. Add the butter and, using your hands, work the butter into the flours with your fingertips until you achieve a coarse crumb. Add the egg yolk, iced water and the vanilla bean paste and lightly knead with the heel of your hand until the pastry just comes together. Flatten into a disc, wrap tightly with plastic wrap and place in the fridge to rest for 1 hour.

Remove from the fridge and roll pastry out on a lightly floured surface, or between two sheets of baking paper, until you have an approximately 30 cm (12 in) round. Transfer to a baking tray lined with baking paper and rest again in the fridge for 30 minutes.

Preheat the oven to 190°C (375°F).

Scoop the quince jam into the centre of the pastry and, using the back of a spoon, roughly spread it out across the circle of pastry, leaving a good 5 cm (2 in) border all the way around. Scatter the raspberries over the top. Using your fingers, fold the pastry over the edge of the fruit mixture, pleating it as you go, and work your way around until the mixture is encased fully around the edge. Remember we are not aiming for pastry chef perfection here; you are simply creating a dam to prevent a fruit spill. No one wants an oven flood. Looks are irrelevant, make the edges purposeful and the rest will take care of itself.

Combine the yolk, cream, cardamom and sugar in a bowl then brush generously all over the pastry edge. Scatter over the raw sugar. Bake until the pastry is golden in colour and the fruit looks to be bubbling, 20–30 minutes.

Serve hot with ice cream or cream and enjoy the happiness it brings.

Slow-roasted Moroccan quince lamb with herby couscous

This lamb is so hands-off in the preparation it feels almost lazy, even though it absolutely isn't. The meat is cooked until it fully surrenders, offering a rich mouthfeel that comes with any lamb that has been well-acquainted with time and an oven. **Serves 6**

1 lamb shoulder (approx. 1.7 kg/ 3 lb 12 oz), at room temperature

1 onion, roughly chopped

2 garlic cloves

2 teaspoons ground cinnamon

2 teaspoons ground cumin

2 teaspoons ground coriander

1 teaspoon ground ginger

1 teaspoon saffron threads

1 tablespoon honey

3 tablespoons olive oil

160 g (5½ oz/½ cup) Quince jam (page 238)

750 ml (25½ fl oz/3 cups) chicken stock

250 ml (8½ fl oz/1 cup) white wine

Whipped feta

120 g (4½ oz/½ cup) crumbled Persian feta

125 g (4½ oz/½ cup) thick Greek yoghurt

Preheat the oven to 150°C (300°F).

For the whipped feta, add the feta and yoghurt to a bowl and whisk vigorously with a fork until combined and the mixture is light and creamy. Set aside in the fridge, but bring to room temperature about 15 minutes before serving.

Place the lamb in a high-sided roasting dish with a relatively snug fit.

Place the onion, garlic cloves, spices, honey and olive oil in a blender and blitz to a rough paste. Turn out into a bowl, add the quince jam and stir to incorporate. Rub the mixture over the top of the lamb in the roasting dish.

Pour the stock and wine around the base of the lamb – it should come up the sides but not cover any of the beautiful marinade you have pressed onto the top of the lamb. Cover tightly with foil and roast for 6 hours, checking on the level of liquid at around 4 hours. If too much has evaporated, add more stock or wine and continue to cook.

Remove the foil for the last 20 minutes of cooking so the marinade can form more of a crust. Set the lamb aside to rest for 15 minutes while you prepare the herby couscous.

Place a frying pan over medium heat. Add the butter and, once hot, cook the onion until soft. Add the spices and couscous and cook, stirring constantly until it looks lightly browned. This adds a lovely nuttiness and helps prevent the couscous from sticking together. Add the stock, a cup or so at a time, waiting until it has been absorbed before adding another, stirring regularly, 5-7 minutes.

Strain and add to a bowl and season generously with salt and freshly ground black pepper. Allow to cool slightly then stir through the lemon zest, nuts and herbs. Toss to combine.

Herby couscous

30 g (1 oz) unsalted butter

1 onion, finely diced

1 teaspoon each cumin seeds and
   coriander seeds, roughly crushed

230 g (8 oz) Israeli couscous

625 ml (21 fl oz/) chicken stock

75 g (2¾ oz/½ cup) pistachio
   kernels, roughly chopped

80 g (2¾ oz/⅓ cup) smoked
   almonds, roughly chopped

½ cup flat-leaf (Italian) parsley
   leaves, chopped

½ cup coriander (cilantro) leaves,
   chopped

¼ cup mint leaves, chopped

¼ cup dill fronds, coarsely torn

finely grated zest of 1 unwaxed
   lemon

To serve

coriander (cilantro) leaves,
   to scatter

generous pinch aleppo pepper
   per serve

pomegranate arils

Add the couscous to serving plates and top with some lamb – it
should just collapse under the pressure of your fork – and finish
with a dollop of whipped feta and some coriander leaves. Sprinkle
over aleppo pepper and pomegranate arils. Serve warm.

Hack

- If you have run out of quince jam and the winter season isn't
  on your doorstep, you can substitute with quince paste at a
  pinch. It's never as good but it does mean you can make this
  dish all year long.

Quince-addled Persian love cakes

These gluten-free beauties are a one-bowl mixing situation and the kind of cake that benefits from sitting overnight, satisfying your pre-emptive baking needs. **Makes 12**

85 g (3 oz) unsalted butter

240 g (8½ oz) ground almonds

135 g (5 oz) rapadura sugar

135 g (5 oz) brown sugar

50 g (1¾ oz) buckwheat flour

1 teaspoon salt

165 g (⅔ cup) Greek yoghurt

3 organic free-range egg yolks

1 small organic free-range egg

1 teaspoon ground cardamom

2 teaspoons vanilla bean paste

½ teaspoon Quince jam (page 238) per cake

To serve

icing (confectioners') sugar, to dust (optional)

Preheat the oven to 180°C (360°F). Grease and line a 12-hole financier tin or brownie tin.

Add the butter to a small saucepan over low heat. Watching carefully, cook until the butter takes on a dark golden hue. You want to brown the butter not burn it, if you take it too far, it will add a bitter taste, which is not what you want. Set aside to cool.

Place the remaining ingredients in a large bowl. Add the cooled browned butter liquid. Using a whisk, lightly combine the ingredients until they are just incorporated – be careful not to overwork the batter here. Spoon the batter into the moulds until they are three-quarters full. Bang the tin gently on the work bench to level the cakes then, delicately, using a teaspoon, dollop a little quince jam in the middle of each cake.

Bake until the cakes are golden and they spring back to the touch when pressed gently, about 25–30 minutes. They will still be quite spongy to the touch; this is what you want.

Allow to cool inside the tin for at least 30 minutes before unmoulding them. Serve as they are or dust lightly with icing sugar.

If you make these ahead, ensure they are at room temperature before dusting with icing sugar and serving to prevent a weird congealed icing mix sitting atop your baked glory.

Index

Acknowledgements

To you the reader. THANK YOU. If I didn't have you, my job as I know it wouldn't exist. I am so thankful for your support, the time you spend cooking my recipes and the food loving community we have created.

Lu, Claude, Eds. My girls. This book is for you. They all are really. You will probably end up using them as doorstops but I hope they carry the memories: of cooking together, of jostling over who will crack the eggs or lick the spoon, of the difficulty and the joy that comes with a working mum when you are small and all you want is my time. It is such a heart bending privilege to be your mum.

Slaughtz. BFG. Best friend. The most skilled last-minute ingredient sorcerer and biggest supporter of all time. Thank you for everything. And I mean EVERYTHING.

Mum and Dad: For everything. Always. Every day.

Michael Harry: The holder of hands. The motivator. Style maven. The best title fighter. Thank you for being so invested. I can't quantify the gimlets I owe you for bringing this book to life and couldn't think of a better publisher to have in my corner. You truly are the very best there is.

Roxy Ryan: Thank you for staying the course. Thank you for the covid zoom chats, and for keeping the dream of this one alive. Your warmth and generosity are unending. Thank you feels insufficient.

Milton Mafia: One of the greatest surprises of motherhood is the village it provides. Thank you for the taste testing, feedback, being an unpaid PR team, the constant sanity checking, the child wrangling and the unending support.

Antonietta Anello: Thank you. For showing us all how to get the nitty-gritty done with ease. Thank you for your constant support and insightful feedback - it's this that makes a book the best it can be.

Ariana Klepac. Here is to bedside chicken salt stashes for ever. Thank you for your keen eye, for keeping the personality with the words and being available at all hours of the day.

Kait Barker and Laura Edrich: Thank you for the snaps. All of them. And doing it again and again until we get the kind of shots I will treasure forever. You both have been on this book making malarkey since the beginning and I couldn't think of two greater talents. Thank you both so much for capturing the kind of "framers" I would save from a burning building.

Vaughan Mossop and the Hardie Grant design team: Thank you for visual and functional perfection. Thank you for creating the kind of book people will want to pull from the shelves.

Published in 2023 by Hardie Grant Books, an imprint of Hardie Grant Publishing

Hardie Grant Books (Melbourne)
Wurundjeri Country
Building 1, 658 Church Street
Richmond, Victoria 3121

Hardie Grant Books (London)
5th & 6th Floors
52–54 Southwark Street
London SE1 1UN

hardiegrant.com/au/books

Hardie Grant acknowledges the Traditional Owners of the country on which we work, the Wurundjeri people of the Kulin nation and the Gadigal people of the Eora nation, and recognises their continuing connection to the land, waters and culture. We pay our respects to their Elders past and present.

A catalogue record for this book is available from the National Library of Australia

A catalogue record for this book is available from the National Library of Australia

From Salt to Jam
ISBN 978 1 74379 890 4

10 9 8 7 6 5 4 3 2 1

Publisher: Michael Harry
Project Editor: Antonietta Anello
Editor: Ariana Klepac
Design Manager: Kristin Thomas
Designer: Vaughan Mossop
Typesetter: Hannah Schubert
Production Manager: Todd Rechner
Production Coordinator: Jessica Harvie

Colour reproduction by Splitting Image Colour Studio
Printed in China by Leo Paper Products LTD.

The paper this book is printed on is from FSC®-certified forests and other sources. FSC® promotes environmentally responsible, socially beneficial and economically viable management of the world's forests.